Explicit Business Writing

Best Practices for the Twenty-First Century

R. Craig Hogan, Ph.D.
The Business Writing Center

BWC Publications
Normal, Illinois

Contact:

Publications
The Business Writing Center
2 Payne Place
Normal, IL 61761
800 827-3770
publications@businesswriting.com

Order copies from this Web address: http://explicit.businesswriting.com.

ISBN 0-9770692-0-6

Printed in the United States

Contents

Introduction

The College Board's survey of 120 major American corporations, employing nearly 8 million people, concluded that writing is a threshold skill for hiring and promotion. Half of the companies surveyed reported that they consider writing ability when making promotion decisions. One manager remarked, "People who cannot write and communicate clearly will not be hired, and if already working, are unlikely to last long enough to be considered for promotion." Another commented, "You can't move up without writing skills" (*Writing: A Ticket to Work . . . Or a Ticket Out. A Survey of Business Leaders* [New York: The College Board, 2004]).

In 2005, the National Commission on Writing asked the human resource directors of state governments, representing 2.7 million state government employees, about the importance of writing skills for employees in the public sector. All reported that writing is an important responsibility for employees, and 75 percent said they take writing into account when hiring (*Writing: A Powerful Message from State Government* [New York: The College Board, 2005]).

Stephen Reder, of the U.S. Department of Education and Portland State University, found that among people with two-year or four-year degrees, the average earnings of workers in the top 20 percent of writing ability are three times as high as workers whose writing falls into the worst 20 percent ("The High Cost of Living and Not Writing Well" [*Fortune,* 7 Dec. 1998], 244).

Clearly, your writing competence is important to you professionally and personally.

Your writing competence is important to your company as well. The primary method of communicating in business today is through writing. Written communication is the infrastructure that connects all the individuals in a business or agency to form a functioning, successful whole. If the written communication infrastructure creates consistently accurate communication, the company or agency prospers. If it regularly fails, the organization suffers.

When you improve your writing ability, you and your company reap the rewards of your competence. Even if others have told you for years that your writing isn't good, you can learn to write so others will remark that your writing is excellent. You just need to know the skills.

Many business writers don't write well for three reasons:

1. Businesses haven't given schools and colleges guidelines for the writing skills employees must have, so writing teachers and professors don't have clear direction about the writing skills to teach. Without clear direction, they use journalism and creative writing as the bases for their writing instruction rather than explicit writing that achieves business objectives.

2. People conform to the styles of writing commonly used in their companies or agencies. Most are based on the old journalism and creative writing guidelines blended with an outmoded business style that uses stilted, archaic phrasing and long, complex sentences. A unique, explicit business writing style that achieves business objectives has been emerging, but most business people are not aware of it. Also, the unique style emerging has not completed its evolution away from journalism, creative writing, and archaic styles to a style with its own identity and methods.

3. The quality of writing in businesses has steadily declined over the last few decades, especially since the advent of e-mail. We now accept confusing, unclear, incomplete, grammatically incorrect, carelessly drafted e-mail as an unavoidable irritation we must live with. Instead, we should expect and deliver explicit writing in all documents, especially e-mail, resulting in 100 percent comprehension by 100 percent of the readers 100 percent of the time.

In this book, I explain the best practices that produce explicit business documents. These best practices use methods that are different from those used in journalism and creative writing; they will enable you to achieve business objectives through explicit writing.

I have taught writing for 35 years, first as a high school English teacher, then as a writing professor at two universities, and eventually as a professor of business writing in a college of business. Between teaching positions, I was a senior staff writer in a consulting company that wrote documents for businesses, the owner of a business-writing-services company, and the manager of communications in a company.

Today, I am the director of The Business Writing Center where I evaluate business writing every day, training business writers from around the world. I know the skills that result in explicit business writing and have been teaching them for decades, refining the skills with every e-mail, memo, letter, and report I evaluate.

This book presents new perspectives on business writing, some of which you may have difficulty accepting fully at first. However, I encourage you to follow the best practices even though at times you may feel they require more than is necessary to make your writing clear. After learning these best practices, you can decide which to apply to a specific document. Eventually, I hope you will value them enough to make them part of your normal practice. I assure you that you and your readers will both benefit if you do so.

The book includes very little about correct English usage (grammar, punctuation, and spelling) because most of the usage problems business people display do not affect the clarity of the message. I am not suggesting that following the rules of grammar, punctuation, and spelling is not important. *It is extremely important.* However, focusing on it would dilute my effort to help you write 100 percent clear documents 100 percent of the time for 100 percent of the readers.

If you are a manager or upper-level executive seeking to improve written communication in your company or agency, begin by reading Chapter 11, "Advice for managers who want employees to write explicit business documents." That chapter explains what you can do to improve your employees' writing and methods that will not work. You may arrange with The Business Writing Center to obtain the original electronic files of this book so you can customize it to your company's or agency's unique needs. Read the explanation at http://explicit.businesswriting.com, or send an e-mail to The Business Writing Center at publications@businesswriting.com asking about that arrangement.

The Business Writing Center offers training in the best practices and in a variety of specialized areas of writing. You can read about the training at http://businesswriting.com. The course catalog is at http://tasks.com. You may post questions on the forum at http://explicit.businesswriting.com.

Style Notes

Sexist pronouns

This book focuses on individual readers and writers, so I must occasionally use singular personal pronouns ("he," "she," "him," "her," "his," and "hers"). To avoid the sexist masculine pronouns and distracting substitutes that cause readers to stumble ("(s)he," "he/she," and "he or she"), I alternate between using masculine and feminine pronouns.

In the near future, the plural pronouns ("they," "them," and "their"), will become acceptable for use in place of singular masculine pronouns in business writing. They are already acceptable as substitutes for singular masculine pronouns in informal conversation, and some companies have given their employees permission to use the plural pronouns for singular nouns in formal business documents.

Spelling "e-mail" with a hyphen

Business writers are writing the word "e-mail" in two ways: "e-mail" and "email." The normal evolution in spelling when people begin to use words in combination (compound words) is from hyphenating the words to joining them without hyphenation, so "email" likely will become the accepted spelling. Now, however, both are acceptable. I have chosen to write "e-mail."

Use of the plural "e-mails"

Some business writers suggest that "e-mail" should be treated like the word "mail," making the plural, "e-mails," unacceptable just as "mails" is unacceptable. However, since "mail" has no plural form, people use "letter" to refer to an article of mail. "E-mail" can be used as "mail" is, to refer to the medium, but it can also be used as "letter" is, to refer to one or several messages. As a result, "e-mails" is becoming as acceptable as "letters" in English. I write "e-mails" in this book.

Using a comma before "and" in a series

Virtually all style guides now agree that business writers should put the comma before "and" in a series of items. *The Chicago Manual of Style*, the recognized authority on English usage, states,

> In a series consisting of three or more elements, the elements are separated by commas. When a conjunction joins the last two elements in a series, a comma is used before the conjunction (*The Chicago Manual of Style* [15th ed. Chicago: University of Chicago Press, 2003], 173).

Grammarians use this as an example of how omitting the comma causes confusion: "In his acceptance speech, he thanked his parents, Mother Theresa and the Pope." A comma before "and" simply makes lists clearer. I mention that here only because some business writers still resist that commonsense use of the comma.

Using two blank spaces between sentences

The trend in business writing is toward using one blank space at the ends of sentences rather than two blank spaces, following the lead of publications that use fully justified text. Fully justified text expands the spaces between words to stretch the lines to the right margin, giving publications their characteristic blocked look.

Unfortunately, the two-space gap between sentences in fully justified publications sometimes results in distractingly large spaces between the sentences when the word processor expands gaps to stretch the text to the right margin. The blank characters also displace a word or two that could fit in the line if they weren't present, so publications, sensitive to the number of pages their works occupy, prefer to devote the space to additional words.

However, for e-mail and other text that is not fully justified, the consensus seems to be that inserting two blank spaces makes the sentence breaks clearer and reduces the dense look of the text, so business writers are inserting two spaces between sentences in text that is not fully justified.

This book breaks with publishing tradition by not using fully justified text because text with varying line lengths is easier to read and justified text provides no benefits for readers. This decision is not an effort to set a trend or make a statement. It is simply in keeping with the central theme of this book: *Business writers must always strive to use writing methods they believe will result in explicit communication.* I know the two blank spaces between sentences will not interfere with reading, and I believe varied line lengths and two blank spaces between sentences make the text easier to read, so I use two blank spaces between sentences and do not use full justification.

PART 1

Explicit Business Writing
Best Practices

Chapter 1

Models of explicit business documents

Five models of explicit business writing follow: an e-mail, a letter, a memo, and two versions of a short report. They illustrate the best practices explained in this book that any business writer can use to create 100 percent clear documents for 100 percent of the readers 100 percent of the time. Explanations of the best practices follow four of the models. The remainder of this book presents explanations of how to use the best practices to create the writing these models exemplify.

Explicit e-mail

The writer of this e-mail assumed the reader's e-mail system would show typography and formatting, so she chose to use the HTML format.

From:	Jean Bosher
To:	Ben Hendrickson
Cc:	
Subject:	Digital video player–answers to your questions

Hello Ben,

Thanks for your helpful e-mail explaining your department's plans for the new digital video system. As always, your explanation was clear and provided what we need.

You asked me two questions about the digital video player:

1. How will the digital video player work with various types of digital video?

2. What are our plans for having the system ready by January?

My answers follow. I understand your comment about needing non-technical explanations to pass along to others in your department. Let me know whether the following explanations work for you. Your comments will help me now and in the future to provide useful explanations for your new-products group.

1. **How will the digital video player work with various types of digital video?**

    The digital video player will play various types of digital video by transforming the video it receives into a form it can play. To do this, the system will contain six programs we call "templates" that will change the video entering the player into the type of information the player can use to show the video. When the player receives the video from any source, it will determine which template will change the video to a form it can play, then run the video through the template and send the changed video to the monitor so it displays perfectly.

    If you would like to know more about the templates, let me know. I can also give you a more technical explanation of how they work.

2. **What are our plans for having the system ready by January?**

    These are the steps in our plan to ensure that the system is ready by January:

    a. Our group will finish the design and begin programming on September 15.

    b. We will finish the programming by November 1.

    c. We will test the player during November to ensure that it functions with the various video sources.

    d. During December, we will place the new program into the same units we have been using for the D4 players and test them to be sure they function properly.

    e. On January 4, we will meet with you for a final review of the product and discussions about marketing.

Let me know if you need any other information. We're looking forward to working with you to create a great product.

Jean Bosner
jean.bosner@blueview.com
X3482

Best practices used in the e-mail

The writer used all of the writing techniques in the right column of the table that follows. The number may seem daunting, but once you know the best practices, you will be able to use these techniques quickly and easily. They will come naturally to you. To help you follow the notes, the original text is in the left column.

Text in the e-mail	Explanation of the best practices
Subject: Digital video player– answers to your questions	1. The subject line contains the key term the reader will recognize and probably use to retrieve the e-mail later, if necessary. It contains words describing what is in the e-mail that will be of interest to the reader.
Hello Ben, Thanks for your helpful e-mail explaining your department's plans for the new digital video system. As always, your explanation was clear and provided what we need.	2. The e-mail begins with a cordial salutation and genuine thanks for something the reader did. That helps build the sense of working as a team and lets the reader know what he did that helped the writer so the reader will more likely repeat the helpful behavior. 3. It states that the reader's previous e mail was clear and helpful. Feedback on the quality of e-mails helps everyone adjust them to fit the reader's needs. It contributes to a corporate culture of expecting quality in writing.
You asked me two questions about the digital video player: 1. How will the digital video player work with various types of digital video? 2. What are our plans for having the system ready by January?	4. The writer explains why the reader is receiving this now. Even if this e-mail is in direct response to the reader's request, this statement ensures that the reader recalls the request. The reader should not have to refer to another e-mail or the thread of e-mails at the end to remember why he is receiving this e-mail.

	5. The e-mail states the reader's request exactly as the reader worded it, listing the two questions the reader asked using the reader's words.
	6. The writer separates her restatement of the reader's questions with blank lines and indents them to make them clearer.
My answers follow.	7. The writer states the contents of this e-mail: "My answers follow."
I understand your comment about needing non-technical explanations to pass along to others in your department. Let me know whether the following explanations work for you. Your comments will help me now and in the future to provide useful explanations for your new-products group.	8. The writer restates the condition the reader imposed: a non-technical explanation. 9. The writer asks for feedback about her explanation to learn whether it fits the reader's needs and to encourage the reader to provide feedback freely. That enables the writer to learn how to write for her reader, ensures the reader is receiving what he wants, and helps create a corporate climate in which people freely give one another feedback on writing. It also shows the reader that this writer is genuinely concerned with giving him what he wants.
1. **How will the digital video player work with various types of digital video?** *The digital video player will play various types of digital video by transforming the video it receives into a form it can play. To do this, the system will contain six programs we call "templates" that will change*	10. The writer breaks for each new thought so the reader can follow the message easily. 11. The writer states the first question on a line by itself, bolded and indented, to act as a heading for the explanation that follows. It is written exactly as the introduction stated it, which is exactly as the reader asked it. The question begins with a number.

the video entering the player into the type of information the player can use to show the video. When the player receives the video from any source, it will determine which template will change the video so it can play it, then run the video through the template and send the resulting video to the monitor so it displays perfectly. *If you would like to know more about the templates, let me know. I can also give you a more technical explanation of how they work.*	12. The writer indents her explanation to the level of the bolded question to display it as an answer to the question. 13. The non-technical explanation uses plain English words. The writer has judged that the reader should know what "template" means for future use in their dialogues, so she presents it and defines it. 14. The writer uses the exact number, "six," for the templates rather than a vague term such as "several" or "some." Business writing should always use exact numbers when the numbers are known. 15. The explanation repeats key terms without changing them: "digital video player," "types of digital video," "transforming," "templates," and later, "the system." 16. The writer offers a more technical explanation if the reader wants it rather than including the technical explanation, which would have added bulk to the message.

2. **What are our plans for having the system ready by January?**
 	
These are the steps in our plan to ensure that the system is ready by January:
 	
    a. Our group will finish the design and begin programming on September 15.
 	
    b. We will finish the programming by November 1.
	17. The writer breaks for the second question and repeats it exactly as it appeared in the introduction and in the reader's request.
	
	18. An opening to the list identifies what is in it: "steps in our plan."
	
	19. The writer breaks the steps in the plan into an indented, numbered list using lowercase letters as the second-level list markers.
	
	20. All sentences in the steps are complete sentences with no words omitted. They begin with capitals and end with periods.

c. *We will test the player during November to ensure that it functions with the various types of video sources.* d. *During December, we will place the new program into the same units we have been using for the D4 players and test them to be sure they function properly.* e. *On January 4, we will meet with you for a final review of the product and discussions about marketing.*	21. The writer skips blank lines between the items in the list to make them clearer. 22. Sentences are clear, straightforward, and generally short. The writer uses capitals and punctuation as she would use for any business document. 23. The explanations use plain, everyday language the writer might use if speaking.
Let me know if you need any other information. We're looking forward to working with you to create a great product.	24. The document ends with an offer to provide more information if the reader wants it and a cordial closing.
Jean Bosner *jean.bosner@blueview.com* *X3482*	25. The writer includes contact information so the reader can contact her easily.

Explicit letter

The following explicit letter uses the best practices.

FRC Financial Services

August 1, 2005

Mr. Simon Strauss, President
Billmont Glass and Ceramics, Inc.
32 Dawson Street
Champaign, IL 61820

Dear Mr. Strauss:

On July 15, you arranged with us to examine the data from your glass container division to see why it appeared to have had a small loss during the first two quarters of 2005 while the division manager said that it had made a small profit. She said she thought it had made a profit because of the increase in sales during the period.

Our analysis revealed that, although the division showed an increase in sales, the profit-and-loss balance was negative. This letter explains how we came to that conclusion. The detailed analysis is attached.

We completed our analysis in three steps:

1. Calculating the total revenue for the first two quarters of 2005

2. Assembling and totaling the expenses for the first two quarters

3. Creating a profit-and-loss statement based on revenue and expenses

Calculating the total revenue for the first two quarters of 2005

We used the accounts receivable records to calculate the revenue for the first two quarters of 2005. We found that strong sales resulted in revenue greater than that recorded for the same period in 2004.

As we examined the records, we learned that the number of returns during the period was nearly twice the number during the first two

---

quarters of 2004. When we subtracted the losses resulting from the large number of returned items, we discovered that the revenue minus losses figure was less than the figure the division manager had been using to evaluate the profit for the period.

Assembling and totaling the expenses for the first two quarters

We then assembled the records for expenses during the first two quarters and totaled them. We used only expense money actually paid out, not money for expenses incurred but not yet paid. Using only expense money paid out helped us keep the figures focused on activity during the two quarters. Our expense records matched the expense records the division manager was using.

Creating a profit-and-loss statement based on revenue and expenses

Finally, we created a profit-and-loss statement based on revenue and expenses. It is attached to this letter. Because the revenue figures that included losses from returned items were lower than those the division manager used, the expenses exceeded revenue by a small amount.

Conclusion

When the total amount refunded for the large number of returns was included in the profit-and-loss analysis, the balance showed a slight loss for the division.

Please contact me if you have any questions about the analysis in this letter or detailed figures in the attached profit-and-loss statement. My phone number is 309 523-5234.

Sincerely,

Larry L. Christian
Senior Accountant

Best practices used in the letter

The writer used all of the writing techniques in the right column of the table that follows. To help you follow the notes, the original text is in the left column.

Text in the letter	Explanation of the best practices
On July 15, you arranged with us to examine the data from your glass container division to see why it appeared to have had a small loss during the first two quarters of 2005 while the division manager said that it had made a small profit. She said she thought it had made a profit because of the increase in sales during the period.	1. The writer opens the body by reminding the reader of why he is receiving this letter now. It contains enough detail to inform the reader, but not more than is necessary. 2. The writer devotes the first sentence to a single thought, putting what the division manager said into its own sentence. The writer knew that sentences should average around 15 to 20 words and that adding words would increase the likelihood that the reader would become confused. 3. Instead of writing "She said **that** because of . . ." the writer wrote, "She said **it made a profit** because of . . ." Use of pronouns such as "that" can easily cause confusion. Writing the words referred to rather than "that" makes the writing explicit. 4. The writer states the problem exactly as the reader explained it to him, both to allow the reader to check the accuracy of the writer's understanding and to let the reader know that the writer understands the problem.
Our analysis revealed that, although the division showed an increase in sales, the profit-and-loss balance was negative. This letter explains how we came to that conclusion. The detailed analysis is attached.	5. The writer presents the conclusion close to the beginning of the letter. 6. The writer breaks for the paragraph that states the conclusion because of the importance of the statement. 7. The paragraph ends with a statement of the contents of the letter. 8. The writer explains the contents of the attachment in the introduction so the reader can decide what to do with it as he reads the letter.

We completed our analysis in three steps:	9. The writer explicitly states the steps in the analysis that the letter explains.
1. Calculating the total revenue for the first two quarters of 2005	10. The steps are broken out into an indented, numbered list rather than being presented in a paragraph.
2. Assembling and totaling the expenses for the first two quarters	11. The writer introduces the list with the exact number of items, "three," and a name for the items: "steps."
3. Creating a profit-and-loss statement based on revenue and expenses	12. Blank lines separate the items in the list because they wrap to two lines.
	13. All words necessary to make complete, clear statements are included in the items. The writer does not drop words such as articles ("a," "an," and "the") to make the items shorter.
	14. The first item in the list refers to "2005" rather than simply "this year" to be explicit.
	15. The list items all begin with "ing" words (gerunds) to be consistent.
Calculating the total revenue for the first two quarters of 2005 *We used the accounts receivable records to calculate the revenue for the first two quarters of 2005. We found that strong sales resulted in revenue greater than that recorded for the same period in 2004.*	16. Headings are important in letters as well as reports. The writer uses the identical terms from the numbered list in the beginning to create headings.
	17. The heading is bolded and has blank space before and after it.
	18. The opening sentence repeats the key words from the introduction and heading: "calculate the revenue for the first two quarters of 2005."
As we examined the records, we learned that the number of returns during the period was nearly twice the number during the first two quarters of 2004. When we subtracted the	19. Most sentences contain no more than one or two ideas and average 18 words.
	20. Most words contain no more than two syllables. That increases the readability of the writing.

losses resulting from the large number of returned items, we discovered that the revenue minus losses figure was less than the figure the division manager had been using to evaluate the profit for the period.	21. The words are ordinary vocabulary someone might use in speaking. The readability level is at about Grade 11 so this executive will be able to understand it easily.
	22. The writer uses clear, simple, straightforward sentences with few interruptions within the sentences.
	23. Information appears in clear paragraph blocks separated by blank lines.
	24. Each of the sections explaining a major point ends with a conclusion. Ending with a conclusion results in a clear, informative, consistent organization that helps readers follow and understand the points.
Assembling and totaling the expenses for the first two quarters	25. The second major point opens with a heading that repeats the statement in the introduction, word for word.
We then assembled the records for expenses during the first two quarters and totaled them. We used only expense money actually paid out, not money for expenses incurred but not yet paid. Using only expense money paid out helped us keep the figures focused on activity during the two quarters. Our expense records matched the expense records the division manager was using.	26. The format is consistent so readers can see the blocks of thought easily.
	27. The writer freely uses personal pronouns: "we," "you," "me," and "my." Explicit business writing uses personal pronouns as freely as they are used in speaking.
	28. The writer chose to write "**Using only expense money paid out** helped us" rather than "**That** helped us," realizing that using the full statement ensures that the writing is clear.

Creating a profit-and-loss statement based on revenue and expenses *Finally, we created a profit-and-loss statement based on revenue and expenses. It is attached to this letter. Because the revenue figures that included losses from returned items were lower than those the division manager used, the expenses exceeded revenue by a small amount.*	29. The writer opens the third point using the same format as the previous two. 30. The opening sentence uses "Finally" as a transition to help the reader follow the explanation. 31. The opening sentence uses the same key terms used in the heading and introduction list: "created a profit and loss statement based on the revenue and expenses." 32. The writer refers to the attachment again because it is relevant to this explanation.
Conclusion *When the total amount refunded for the large number of returns was included in the profit-and-loss analysis, the balance showed a slight loss for the division.*	33. The writer uses the heading, "Conclusion," to make the conclusion statement explicit. The heading is separated from the text by blank lines before and after. 34. The conclusion is stated both in the beginning and in the "Conclusion" section.
Please contact me if you have any questions about the analysis in this letter or detailed figures in the attached profit-and-loss statement. My phone number is 309 523-5234.	35. The writer ends cordially, with an invitation for the reader to contact him. Including his phone number in the closing paragraph emphasizes his willingness to talk about the analysis and conclusion.

Explicit memo

The following memo uses the best practices explained in this book.

DATE: August 21, 2005

TO: Sally, Fred, May, and Lester

FROM: Linda Tray

SUBJECT: VERY IMPORTANT - New city travel form

Dear Sally, Fred, May, and Lester:

I know you're busy just keeping up with the field offices, but we're going to have to fill out another form. This memo explains what the form is and how to fill it out. Call me after you've read this so I can answer questions you may have about it.

The city's Taxation Department is going to tax the travel agencies, so we need to report to them any travel expenses we remit to our two travel agencies.

**You must fill out a form with expenses for
each travel agency you use for each trip.**

The form is attached. The procedure for filling it out follows.

Contact information

In the "Contact Information" area, write your name, phone number, and position as indicated.

Travel information

In the "Travel Information" area, write the following:

Departure	Write "Houston." They want only the city name.
Destination	The city name and state to which you are traveling. If you are going to more than one city during a single trip, list each separately (example: Chicago, Illinois; Peoria, Illinois).
Mode of travel	Select "auto" or "plane."
Agency costs	Write only costs directly payable to the agency.

Travel Agency Information

In the "Travel Agency Information" area, write either Sunrise Travel or Corporate Travel Services, depending on which agency you use. Fill in their addresses from the information on your travel report. If you use both agencies for a trip, you must fill out one form for each agency.

That's all we have to do, but we have to do it so our administration doesn't receive a phone call from City Hall.

Call me after you've read this.

Linda

Best practices used in the memo

The writer used all of the writing techniques in the right column of the table that follows. To help you follow the notes, the original text is in the left column.

Text in the memo	Explanation of the best practices
VERY IMPORTANT - New city travel form	1. The "SUBJECT" line contains a note indicating the importance of the message. The words could be used later to retrieve this memo.
Dear Sally, Fred, May, and Lester:	2. The writer addresses the individuals by name rather than "Team" to personalize the message.
I know you're busy just keeping up with the field offices, but we're going to have to fill out another form.	3. The writer begins with a cordial opening that empathizes with the readers. That will help diminish the negative reaction to having to fill out another form. This cordial, informal opening and closing are the only informal parts of the memo. The remainder of the memo is strictly business.
This memo explains what the form is and how to fill it out.	4. The writer states the contents of the memo so the reader knows what to expect.

Call me after you've read this so I can answer questions you may have about it.	5. The writer includes a feedback loop to ensure that the reader reads and understands the memo.
The city's Taxation Department is going to tax the travel agencies, so we need to report to them any travel expenses we remit to our two travel agencies.	6. The writer includes a brief rationale for the form without including detail unnecessary for the reader to understand the context.
You must fill out a form with expenses for each travel agency you use for each trip.	7. The writer states important information the reader must remember at the beginning, bolding and indenting it to give it emphasis.
The form is attached. The procedure for filling it out follows.	8. The writer begins the instructions by explaining where to find the form and that the instructions for filling it out are going to follow. That lets the readers know to look at the form as they read through the procedure.
Contact information *In the "Contact Information" area, write your name, phone number, and position as indicated.*	9. The name of each area is presented on a separate line, bolded, with a blank line before and after. The area name matches the name on the form exactly. The text begins with the area name again to be explicit. 10. The explanation is indented to make it clear that the explanation accompanies the area name. 11. The explanation explicitly states all the content the reader might put in the area, rather than simply "Enter your contact information." However, the information for each field is obvious enough that the writer has not explained each field.

Travel information *In the "Travel Information" area, write the following:*	12. The writer maintains a consistent format for presenting the area names and explanations. 13. The list of field names is preceded by an opening statement so the reader knows what will follow.
<u>Departure</u> *Write "Houston." They want only the city name.* <u>Destination</u> *The city name and state to which you are traveling. If you are going to more than one city during a single trip, list each separately (example: Chicago, Illinois; Peoria, Illinois).* <u>Mode of travel</u> *Select "auto" or "plane."* <u>Agency costs</u> *Write only costs directly payable to the agency.*	14. The writer decided that these fields need explanation, so she broke them out into a list with the field name clearly identified and the explanations indented to make them easy to read. 15. The explanation contains all the information the reader needs, with no unnecessary information. 16. The writer includes all words that make clear sentences. She does not drop articles ("a," "an," or "the") or other small words to conserve space. 17. She includes an example to make the "Destination" field explanation clear. 18. She skips blank lines between the field explanations to make them easier to read.
Travel Agency Information *In the "Travel Agency Information" area, write either Sunrise Travel or Corporate Travel Services, depending on which agency you use. Fill in their addresses from the information on your travel report. If you use both agencies for a trip, you must fill out one form for each agency.*	19. She begins all of the area explanations consistently: "In the _____ area, write . . ." Readers understand and remember most successfully when the presentation is in a consistent pattern. 20. The writer specifies the source for information even though that might be obvious to the reader. 21. The writer states the fact that the reader must fill out a travel form for each agency because it is relevant here, even though she already stated that fact early in the memo.

That's all we have to do, but we have to do it so our administration doesn't receive a phone call from City Hall.	22. The writer ends cordially, emphasizing the importance of the activity again. 23. The informal ending explains the consequence without including inappropriate comments about the activity or City Hall.
Call me after you've read this.	24. The writer repeats the action the reader must complete. The action is the feedback that lets the writer know the reader has read and understood the message.

Explicit short report

This short report exemplifies the best practices explained in this book.

Evaluation of the Foxworth eFirm Software
Juan Martinez and Lisa Fitzsimmons

Over the past year, our firm has been searching for an efficient, cost-effective software system that will allow us to manage litigation matters. In March, the firm learned about the Foxworth eFirm software product that seemed to address many of our needs. Since that time, we have been evaluating the software through visits to the developer and contacts with firms presently using it.

As a result of our evaluation of the software, we recommend purchasing it. This report explains the features we identified that the software we purchase must have and our evaluation of the Foxworth eFirm software based on those features.

Features the Software Must Have

In our meetings preparing for this evaluation, we developed a set of features the software product we purchase must have. The software must allow our firm to do all of the following:

- Share information
- Link to eDiscovery resources
- Manage document storage and retrieval
- Monitor document production
- Present information flexibly for trial preparation

- Manage new Web-based resources as we add them
- Manage time tracking and billing

All of these features must be available to both our internal and external team members.

Our Evaluation of the Foxworth eFirm Software Based on the Features

We evaluated the Foxworth eFirm software to determine whether it offers the features we agreed the software must have. Our assessment for each feature follows:

Share information. The Foxworth eFirm software will permit us to share case calendars, contact lists, and task lists through our intranet and extranet, making the resources available to internal and external team members.

Link to eDiscovery resources. The software will permit all team members to link to information resources available over the Internet.

Manage document storage and retrieval. It will provide a library of discovery documents, pleadings, correspondence, memos and any other documents or images we place into the library. All team members will be able to perform searches by subject, title, or date.

Monitor document production. The software will allow us to monitor every stage of document production: reviewing documents before production, monitoring the production stages, and establishing timelines for the completed documents.

Present information flexibly for trial preparation. The Foxworth software will allow us to organize and present information by issue, subject, or witness through the intranet and extranet.

Manage new Web-based resources as we add them. It will permit us to add Web-based resources without restriction, as they become available.

Manage time tracking and billing. The software will allow us to track time by task and client, providing billing summaries and detail with hours worked by attorney and task for each client.

Our Recommendation

The Foxworth eFirm software has all of the features we identified that we require in an efficient, cost-effective software system. It will also allow internal and external team members to manage litigation matters. We recommend that the firm purchase and implement the software.

Best practices used in the report

The writer used these best practices in the report.

Text in the report	Explanation of the best practices
Over the past year, our firm has been searching for an efficient, cost-effective software system that will allow us to manage litigation matters. In March, the firm learned about the Foxworth eFirm software product that seemed to address many of our needs. Since that time, we have been evaluating the software through visits to the developer and contacts with firms presently using it.	1. The writers have chosen to skip a blank line between the single-spaced paragraphs and indent the first lines of the paragraphs. One or the other is sufficient, but these writers feel both will make the writing more appealing and clearer, so they have used both. 2. The report begins with an introduction that explains why the reader is receiving this now.
As a result of our evaluation of the software, we recommend purchasing it. This report explains the features we identified that the software we purchase must have and our evaluation of the Foxworth eFirm software based on these features.	3. The introduction contains a statement of the recommendation. It is the primary focus of the report and of great interest to the reader. 4. The introduction ends with a statement of the contents of the report. This statement is the writer's contract with the reader.
Features the Software Must Have *In our meetings preparing for this evaluation, we developed a set of features the software product we purchase must have.*	5. The first point immediately follows the statement of contents. 6. The writer introduces the first point with a heading containing the key term from the statement of contents: "features the software must have." 7. The heading has blank lines before and after it for visual clarity. 8. The first sentence after the heading opens the explanation using the key term, "features the software must have." This helps the reader stay oriented to the point of the explanation.

The software must allow our firm to do all of the following: • *Share information* • *Link to eDiscovery resources* • *Manage document storage and retrieval* [list continues here] *All of these features must be available to both our internal and external team members.*	9. The writer breaks the features into a bulleted list and introduces them with an explicit statement. 10. Blank lines before and after the bulleted list items make them easy to read. 11. The writer uses a one-sentence paragraph for the closing thought in the first section. One-sentence paragraphs are useful in explicit business writing.
Our Evaluation of the Foxworth eFirm Software Based on the Features *We evaluated the Foxworth eFirm software to determine whether it offers the features we agreed the software must have. Our assessment for each feature follows:*	12. The second point begins with a heading that uses the identical key terms from the statement of contents presented in the introduction. 13. The first sentence of the point repeats the key terms: "evaluation of the Foxworth eFirm software" and "features." 14. The writer uses the key term, "features," as often as necessary without substituting a synonym.
Share information. *The Foxworth eFirm software will permit us to share case calendars, contact lists, and task lists through our intranet and extranet, making the resources available to internal and external team members.* **Link to eDiscovery resources.** *It will permit all team members to link to pertinent information resources available over the Internet.* [The other features follow.]	15. The features in the evaluation appear in the same order in which the writer presented them in the introduction. 16. The writer precedes each evaluation with the name of the feature in bold, using the identical words for the feature that appeared in the bulleted list. 17. The sentences are clear, straightforward, and direct. 18. The writer uses simple, plain English words.

Our Recommendation *The Foxworth eFirm software has all of the features we identified that we require in an efficient, cost-effective software system. It will also allow internal and external team members to manage litigation matters. We recommend that the firm purchase and implement the software.*	19. The recommendation begins with a bold heading to set it apart. 20. The final paragraph contains a succinct statement of the evaluation followed by the recommendation.

Best practices for formatting explicit documents

Explicit business writing uses visual devices such as lines, indentations, selective bolding, and tables that make the writing easier to follow and understand. The following version of the report contains examples of these devices.

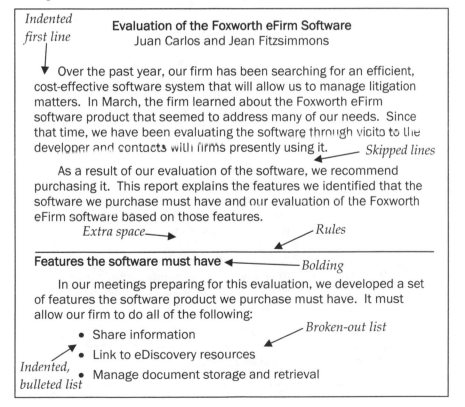

Indented first line

Evaluation of the Foxworth eFirm Software
Juan Carlos and Jean Fitzsimmons

Over the past year, our firm has been searching for an efficient, cost-effective software system that will allow us to manage litigation matters. In March, the firm learned about the Foxworth eFirm software product that seemed to address many of our needs. Since that time, we have been evaluating the software through visits to the developer and contacts with firms presently using it. *— Skipped lines*

As a result of our evaluation of the software, we recommend purchasing it. This report explains the features we identified that the software we purchase must have and our evaluation of the Foxworth eFirm software based on those features.

Extra space ⟶   *Rules*

Features the software must have ⟵ *Bolding*

In our meetings preparing for this evaluation, we developed a set of features the software product we purchase must have. It must allow our firm to do all of the following:

- Share information   *Broken-out list*
- Link to eDiscovery resources
- Manage document storage and retrieval

Indented, bulleted list

- Monitor document production
- Present information flexibly for trial preparation
- Manage new Web-based resources as we add them
- Manage time tracking and billing

These features must be available to both internal and external team members. ◄——————— *One-sentence paragraphs*

Our Evaluation of the Foxworth eFirm Software

We evaluated the Foxworth eFirm software to determine whether it offers the required features. Our assessment for each feature follows: ——— *Bolded key terms*

Share information   The Foxworth eFirm software will permit us
                                   to share case calendars, contact lists, and
                                   task lists through our intranet and extranet,
                                   making the resources available to internal
Indented explanations   and external team members.

Link to eDiscovery   The software will permit all team members
resources   to link to pertinent information resources
                                   available over the Internet.

Manage document   It will provide a library of discovery
storage and retrieval   documents, pleadings, correspondence,
                                   memos and any other documents or
                                   images we place into the library. All team
                                   members will be able to perform searches
                                   by subject, title, or range of dates.

Monitor document   The software will allow us to monitor every
production   stage of document production: reviewing
                                   documents before production, monitoring
                                   the production stages, and establishing
                                   timelines for the completed documents.

Present information   The Foxworth eFirm software will allow us
flexibly for trial   to organize and present information by
preparation   issue, subject, or witness through the
                                   intranet and extranet.

Manage new Web-   It will permit us to add Web-based
based resources as   resources without restriction as they
we add them   become available.

| **Manage time tracking and billing** | The software will allow us to track time by task and client, providing billing summaries and detail with hours worked by attorney and task for each client. |

Our Recommendation

The Foxworth eFirm software has all of the features we identified that we want in an efficient, cost effective software system that will allow internal and external team members to manage litigation matters. We recommend that the firm purchase and implement the software.

By using the best practices described in this book, you will be able to write documents as explicit as these are.

Chapter 2

Best practices for explicit business writing

Any business writer can write explicit e-mails, memos, letters, and reports that communicate clearly and have impact. Over the past decade, as writing has become the predominant method of communication in business, business-writing trainers have identified the characteristics of explicit business writing and the best practices that create them. This part of the book presents the best practices. The rest of the book explains how to use them. If you use these best practices, your writing will be so clear it cannot be misunderstood.

Chapters 13 through 16 contain these best practices rewritten as standards for business writing a company or agency might adopt. You may obtain the electronic files with the standards in them to copy and use freely in your company at http://explicit.businesswriting.com. You may also obtain the electronic files containing all the text of this book to customize to your company's standards using your company's examples. Read about this option at http://explicit.businesswriting.com or send an e-mail to publications@businesswriting.com to ask about it.

E-mail must use the same best practices that apply to memos, letters, and reports.

E-mail has grown to have its own style that differs from memos, letters, and reports. Business people write e-mails as thoughts occur to them and send the e-mail without revising the words into coherent messages. As a result, businesses have come to excuse writing that is fragmented, incomplete, full of careless language errors, and difficult to understand. However, the quality of e-mail writing must improve if e-mails are to communicate without error to 100 percent of the readers 100 percent of the time. The best practices must apply to e-mails as well as memos, letters, and reports.

Best Practices

Plan and organize.

Explicit business writing provides readers with everything they need to achieve the writer's objectives.

1. Have clear objectives.

2. Provide information that suits the reader's knowledge of the subject, educational background, technical expertise, need for concrete explanations, and need for depth of knowledge.

3. Include everything every intended reader needs to achieve your objectives.

4. Respond to requests by providing precisely what the person asked for, under the conditions specified.

5. Give readers the information they need at the specific points where they need it for maximum understanding.

6. When readers have differing needs or abilities, write different versions or sections of the document to match the readers' needs and abilities.

7. Present topics in the same order throughout and link all the contents in each part.

Build the communication infrastructure.

Explicit business writing that achieves objectives fosters a climate of cooperation and an expectation for quality in written communication.

8. In e-mails, letters, and memos, write thanks, commendations, and genuine statements of good will that build teams and partnerships with clients.

9. Present the information with consideration for the reader's possible reaction to the subject and you.

10. Use the tone and level of formality that fit the objectives and the reader.

11. Ask for and give feedback on the clarity and relevance of documents and writing.

Prepare readers to understand and act.

Explicit business writing begins by preparing readers to read with purpose and understanding.

12. Write e-mail subject lines using words that alert the reader to the contents, required action, or critical information in the e-mail.

13. In the introduction, explain everything readers need to know to understand fully why they are receiving the document.

14. In the introduction, describe all actions the reader is expected to perform and any critical information the reader must know.

15. Summarize conclusions and recommendations at the beginning.

16. Write a clear statement of the contents at the end of the introduction so readers know what to expect and can prepare for reading.

Provide a clear framework that guides readers.

Explicit business writing has a clear framework that guides readers through the information

17. Put the information into clearly defined blocks that the reader can read, understand, and remember, one block at a time.

18. For each information block, write an explicit opening statement the reader can use to begin putting the block's details into a framework.

19. For lists with items that are each several paragraphs or pages long, open the lists with statements of the contents and open each list item with a description of the item's contents.

20. For lists with items that are a few lines long, break out the lists with numbers and bullets.

21. Present information in a clear visual blueprint so readers can see the organization as they read.

22. Use tables to organize the information so readers can place the details into a clear framework.

23. End the document with a conclusion that helps readers achieve your objectives.

24. Include feedback loops that reflect the importance of the content and your assessment of the likelihood this reader will understand or act as expected.

Use explicitly clear explanations.

Explicit business writing has explanations that are so clear they cannot be misunderstood.

25. Write concrete, detailed descriptions of problems and issues.

26. Write requests that state directly, unambiguously, and completely what you are requesting.

27. Use key terms consistently.

28. Fully explain the concept behind every new key term as the reader encounters it.

29. Have a clear focus for the document and for each part.

30. Communicate technical subjects clearly to non-technical readers.

31. Write instructions and procedures that are complete and concrete.

32. Provide sufficient, relevant evidence for statements.

Write clear, concise paragraphs, sentences, and words.

Explicit business writing uses clear, concise paragraphs, sentences, and words.

33. Write concisely.

34. Write clear, focused, organized paragraphs that help readers identify, understand, and remember concepts.

35. Write sentences that are complete, simple, clear, and straightforward.

36. Use only simple punctuation.

37. Use words every intended reader will understand.

Write a final draft that has correct usage (grammar, punctuation, and spelling) and uses clear formatting.

Explicit business writing has well-written sentences with correct usage (grammar, punctuation, and spelling) and clear formatting.

38. Polish and proofread all documents.

39. Use formatting that makes the text easy to read.

Chapter 3

What you must do to learn to write explicitly

To write explicitly so your e-mails, memos, letters, and reports are so clear they cannot be misunderstood, you will have to follow nine guidelines:

1. Don't attend a workshop expecting to learn how to write. Writing workshops are too short to teach writing skills and they cannot provide the focus on your own writing that is necessary to learn writing skills.

2. Study the best practices in this book and use them in your writing over the next several months. Invest time in improving your writing with every document you write. When you are first learning the skills in these best practices, you will spend more time writing a document, but once you learn them, you will write even more quickly than you're writing now.

3. If you can, have an in-house trainer work with you to give you feedback and coaching, or enroll in one of The Business Writing Center's online courses at http://businesswriting.com. This book will help you learn the skills without a trainer if you practice the skills over time, but feedback from a trainer can be very helpful.

4. Ask readers whether your writing is clear and whether it provides what they want. Listen to what they say, regardless of the negative comments you may sometimes receive. If all you do is keep throwing messages and never find out if people are catching what you throw, you'll be misunderstood at times, but you won't know it until the misunderstanding causes a problem.

5. You may have to give up on some old practices you learned from your high school English teacher. You're learning how to make readers know, believe, or do what you intend. Nothing else about writing is important. That means you may have one-sentence paragraphs, split infinitives, sentences ending in prepositions, contractions, "I" and "you" throughout, and anything else that will help you get your message across clearly. Some rules your English teacher told you are unbreakable just don't matter in explicit business writing.

6. You have to be willing to write in ways that may feel odd to you. You may believe business writing should look like a magazine article or novel, with long, dense paragraphs, extended sentences that pile ideas on top of each other, and complex, intellectual vocabulary. You'll have to be willing to write shorter paragraphs and sentences, break paragraphs into bulleted or numbered lists, and use the same simple words you would use if you were speaking to someone.

7. You must be willing to give up the outdated, odd language that has been common in law, business, government, and other professions since the nineteenth century. You'll need to clean out the closet and throw away "utilize," "enclosed herein," "aforesaid," "under separate cover," "as per your request," "thanking you in advance," "pursuant to," and all the other old slippers that may feel comfortable to you, but are as archaic as someone sending you a memo on paper written in longhand.

    If you're a lawyer, you have to give up "hereinafter," "dated as of," "shall," "set out therein," "we are in receipt of," "by and through the undersigned," and all the other outmoded vocabulary that dropped out of everyday speech decades or centuries ago. If you are committed to communicating clearly, this language has to go.

8. You will have to write some messages with more care and structure than you're accustomed to. Your e-mail messages should have clear, complete sentences and headings to guide readers. You may feel that e-mail should be a casual, unstructured medium much like friendly speaking. However, e-mail has become too unstructured to communicate clearly. Write e-mail as you would write an explicit letter or report.

9. Most of all, you must be willing to do whatever it takes to communicate successfully. If you don't have the commitment, you won't learn to write so explicitly that every document with your name on it is clear and successful.

After you've finished this book, if you find that you consistently want to go back through your e-mail messages to make sure they are so clear they cannot be misunderstood, then you'll know you've arrived — you have made the commitment to write clearly. However, in the days after you finish this book, if you still send off your e-mails without planning or editing them because you're driven to get on to your next activity, then you're doomed to remain a writing weakling. You can still get some value out of this book by using it as a mouse pad.

Business Writing Center Training

The Business Writing Center offers individualized, competency-based training in the writing best practices through 28 courses, from basic grammar to writing audit reports and grant proposals. The training is delivered by faculty to trainees around the world using the Internet and e-mail for communication. To find out more about the training, visit The Business Writing Center's Web site at http://businesswriting.com.

PART 2

Training in Best Practices for
Explicit Business Writing

Chapter 4

Explicit business writing provides readers with everything they need to achieve the writer's objectives.

When you write an e-mail, memo, letter, or report, you likely have the impulse to just start writing. However, that's inefficient and time consuming because you end up having to reorganize after you've written. Best practices in construction require that the builder start with carefully drawn blueprints. In the same way, to create explicit business writing, you must have the blueprint before you write.

These are the reasons you must plan before writing:

1. Simply writing as thoughts come into your head increases the likelihood that you will not organize your writing well. Most writers can't or don't revise their documents after they finish writing them.

2. Focusing on writing words and sentences before planning your thoughts inhibits your ability to generate the information you need, judge its relevance, and organize it so it has the impact on readers you want it to have. Finish the first step: Generate the information you need to accomplish your objectives. Then explain the information using words and sentences.

3. Writing without planning also creates writer's block. If you find you can't decide how to start e-mails, memos, letters, or reports, it's probably because you don't have a plan that will show you where to start.

Always write notes before you start writing. The best practices for writing notes for explicit business documents follow.

Best Practice

Have clear objectives.

Guidelines for this best practice:

1. Write your objectives in a few words on the first page of the document.

2. The objective with the highest priority is to satisfy the reader's request.

Business writers who have clear objectives for their writing are more successful in having an impact on readers because they are able to determine precisely what the readers need to accomplish the objectives. Having clear business objectives is also the primary way to overcome writer's block.

Write your objectives in a few words on the first page of your document.

Write a few words for each of your objectives at the beginning of your document, listing each on a separate line. When you become accustomed to reviewing your objectives just before you begin to write, you may decide not to write them. However, for longer documents and important messages, writing the objectives will always help you focus on achieving them.

You will return to this list of your objectives regularly. Use the following list of the most common objectives as a guide. The reader will

- receive what he requested
- follow a procedure
- know
- act
- decide
- believe

Following are examples of what the writer might write at the beginnings of an e-mail and a memo:

❖ Example

The writer is preparing to write an e-mail about an upcoming meeting:

know – time, place

believe – this meeting is important

act – be there

❖ Example

The writer is preparing to write a memo convincing people to submit software feedback forms:

know – forms due date

believe – the forms are necessary for us to finish development

act – submit the forms

You will use these brief objectives as guides to help you decide what to include in the document. If you are preparing a long document that is especially important, such as a proposal for funding, you may spend hours defining your objectives and writing them in full sentences. After you finish the document, review the objectives to evaluate whether your document will accomplish them.

The objective with the highest priority is to satisfy the reader's request.

The objective with the highest priority is to provide readers with what they have requested. The request may be in the form of an RFP (request for proposal) or an e-mail asking you to send information about an upcoming meeting. You will be successful if you give the readers what they want, when they want it, under the conditions in which they want it.

Best Practice

Provide information that suits the reader's knowledge of the subject, educational background, technical expertise, need for concrete explanations, and need for depth of knowledge.

Guidelines for this best practice:

1. Know your readers.

2. Evaluate each reader's knowledge of the subject in each objective.

3. Evaluate each reader's educational background.

4. Evaluate each reader's technical expertise.

5. Evaluate the amount of concreteness each reader needs to be able to understand and act.

6. Evaluate the depth of information each reader needs.

Know your readers.

To accomplish your business objectives, you must identify who the readers are and what they need. Follow this procedure after you have written the objectives.

1. Identify the primary reader. Write that person's name below the objectives.

2. Identify the secondary readers who might read the message. You must consider their needs and reactions, so write their names as well.

3. Specify the following for each reader:
   - knowledge of the subject
   - educational background
   - technical expertise
   - need for concrete explanations
   - need for depth

The pages that follow explain each of these reader characteristics.

4. Increase your understanding of your readers over successive communications. Build a more solid communication infrastructure for your own success and your company's or agency's success by fine-tuning your understanding of the readers. Each document contributes to building a communication infrastructure by teaching you about the reader and teaching the reader about you.

5. Solicit feedback from the readers regularly to identify writing that results in 100 percent comprehension by these readers: "Was that explanation I gave you clear? Would you like more detail?" Use the person's response to determine the ideal level of detail for future messages. Keep copies of the documents that have been successful and use them as models.

6. If your team writes regularly for the same readers, learn about them as a team and prepare a guide for current and new team members.

   - Include models of documents that communicate most successfully to these readers.

   - Include lists of your specialized jargon that readers will understand and vocabulary they may not know.

   - Meet occasionally to review and discuss actual documents so you know what others are writing and what they have found to be successful.

Evaluate five reader characteristics for each reader.

Evaluate each reader for these five reader characteristics:

1. Knowledge of the subject in each objective

2. Educational background

3. Technical expertise in the subject of the document

4. Level of concreteness each reader needs

5. Depth of information each reader needs

If you have several readers or several types of readers who have the same characteristics, you should have one set of evaluations for each reader or type of reader. Before you write your notes for a document, review these reader characteristics so you can adapt your writing to allow for any characteristics that stand out.

Eventually, you will assess your readers intuitively without thinking about the evaluations. For very important documents, however, you may write the evaluations at the beginnings of the documents.

Evaluation 1: The reader's knowledge of the subject in each objective

Your goal is to achieve 100 percent comprehension by 100 percent of the readers 100 percent of the time. Evaluate each reader's knowledge of the subjects in the objectives to determine the amount of explanation each reader needs. A reader knowledgeable in one area may still need much explanation and many examples in another.

Think of the reader as having one of the following:

- low knowledge
- moderate knowledge
- high knowledge

❖ Example

The writer is preparing to write a report describing what she learned during her investigation of why users aren't using the new software her department prepared for them. Her report will contain her recommendations for taking care of the problem. Her readers are Lennie, an administrator who knows nothing about the software, and Darlene, a systems analyst who helped develop the software.

---

know – the interface is too complicated

believe – we should meet with the users to prepare a new interface

act – provide suggestions about how we should approach the users

> Darlene – Knowledge high
> Lennie – Knowledge low

Evaluation 2: The reader's educational background

The reader's educational background will influence the vocabulary you use and the amount you can teach the reader. A reader you evaluate as low for knowledge, but who has an advanced degree in a related field, will likely need less detail and will understand the jargon fairly quickly. A reader with low knowledge and a high school diploma will likely need more detailed explanations and may not be ready to learn the vocabulary. Make judgments about the content of the document and the way you write it based on these combinations of knowledge and educational background.

Think of the reader as having one of the following:

- a high school diploma or less
- some college coursework or a degree
- advanced degrees

Evaluation 3: The reader's technical expertise

The technical level at which you write the document will depend on the reader, the reader's expectations for this document, and the subject.

Think of the reader as having one of the following:

- low technical expertise
- moderate technical expertise
- high technical expertise

Evaluation 3: The reader's need for concrete explanations to be able to understand and act successfully

A **concrete** explanation has more sense detail: what the reader will see, hear, smell, taste, or touch. For actions, someone with a high need for concrete explanations needs steps with the actions described so explicitly that there can be no misunderstanding.

A **general** explanation allows the reader to fill in details because the writer has confidence this reader will make good judgments, knows the process, and may even formulate a plan of action better than the writer could have suggested. The more the reader knows about the subject and the higher the reader's level of education, the more general the explanations can be. Writing more generally for this reader enables you to write less and partner with the reader.

Usually, a reader with low knowledge will need more concrete details. However, if the document contains actions the reader must perform accurately, or if achieving the objectives is critical to the business, concrete explanations likely will be necessary for any readers, regardless of their knowledge of the subject.

Think of the reader as having one of the following:

- low concrete need
- moderate concrete need
- high concrete need

Evaluation 4: The depth of information the reader needs

"Depth" here refers to the amount of detail or content this reader must have to achieve your objective. For example, a company profile might be two pages long for the reader who wants little depth or 20 pages long for the reader who wants considerable depth. Executive summaries are usually one-tenth the length of the full report for readers who want little depth. The full report is for readers who want considerable depth.

Depth differs from technical complexity. For example, a highly technical report might have little depth but use technical jargon because it is written for a manager with technical expertise who wants only an overview of a project. A second version of the report may include all the depth in the project, but no technical explanations because the intended reader is an executive who must explain the project and answer questions about it, but who has no technical background.

The best practices for writing the sentences and words appropriate for non-technical readers are explained in Chapter 8. Here, only the depth of content is considered so you can decide what information to include in the document.

Think of the reader as needing one of the following:

- little depth
- moderate depth
- considerable depth

❖ Example

For most business documents, review the five reader characteristics and consider any that stand out for a reader. For an important document, you might write your assessments at the beginning, as in this example:

---

know – the interface is too complicated

believe – we should meet with the users to prepare a new interface

act – provide suggestions about how we should approach the users

Darlene –

Knowledge – high
Education – college degree
Technical knowledge – high
Concreteness need – high
Depth need – high

Lennie –

Knowledge – low
Education – college degree
Technical knowledge – low
Concreteness need – low
Depth need – little

Darlene is technically knowledgeable, but has a high concreteness need because she will be involved in the critical activity of changing the software. She needs the details. Lennie has low technical knowledge, but doesn't need the concrete explanations because he requires only an overview of the issues.

These unique perspectives on the readers will help you adjust your writing to their needs. You will use these evaluations of your reader repeatedly as you write using the best practices that follow.

Best Practice

Include everything every intended reader needs
to be able to achieve your objectives.

Guidelines for this best practice:

1. Include only the information that will accomplish the
    business objectives with these readers.

2. Write the central idea(s) in a word or a few words.

3. Words representing concepts are referred to in this book as
    "key terms."

4. Revise the words to make them precise key terms.

5. Write key terms for the main points explaining each
    central idea.

6. Write key terms for the sub-points explaining the
    main points.

7. Write key terms for the remaining levels to the depth the
    reader needs.

8. For documents that have a format, such as an audit report,
    write the major headings for the report, and then work with
    sections one at a time.

9. For instructions and procedures, write key terms for every
    critical action.

10. Revise the words to make them precise key terms
    appropriate for the readers.

Include only the information that will accomplish the business objectives with these readers.

Explicit business writing includes exactly what readers need to
accomplish the business objectives, with no unnecessary information.
Too often, an e-mail or report is so dense with irrelevant information that

the reader doesn't finish it, or it is so incomplete the reader doesn't have enough information to understand it.

The text that follows explains how to select the information that will accomplish your business objectives.

Write the central idea(s) in a word or a few words.

On the first page of your e-mail, memo, letter, or report, write the central idea in capitals using one word or a few words. Bold, center, or capitalize the words. If you have more than one central idea, write a word or few words for each. That would be the case if you were writing an e-mail with three distinct subjects: the Eastern Region's third-quarter revenue, possible candidates for the position of account manager, and the date the new product will be ready for sale. Those three very different subjects represent three central ideas. Nearly all reports have one central idea.

❖ Example

Imagine you're preparing an e-mail for a team whose role is to advise upper-level management about changes that might be needed in the work environment. The e-mail will explain two topics: information about the next meeting and problems employees have encountered with the new scheduling software.

You would write these two central ideas as you started to think through what will be in the e-mail:

INFORMATION ON THE NEXT MEETING

PROBLEMS WITH THE NEW SCHEDULING SOFTWARE

Words representing concepts are referred to in this book as "key terms."

Throughout this book, words that represent concepts important to the document are referred to as "key terms." A key term is any combination of words you use to identify the concept in your mind.

❖ Examples

The key terms are bolded in the sentences that follow. Each key term represents a concept:

> This report explains our **rationale** for **purchasing new assembly equipment.**

> We discovered that the **division losses** were due to **accounting errors.**

The words presented on the previous page as the central ideas for an e-mail are the key terms for the concepts:

> **INFORMATION ON THE NEXT MEETING**

> **PROBLEMS WITH THE NEW SCHEDULING SOFTWARE**

As you can see, often the key terms contain several words or an entire phrase. The key term should include all the words that will identify the concept explicitly for you and the reader. Instead of referring to them as "key words or key phrases," this book simply refers to all the words that identify a concept clearly in your mind as a "key term."

Readers will find your consistent use of key terms very helpful as you use the terms to help them navigate through your explanations.

Write key terms for the main points explaining each central idea.

Explicit business writing has clearly defined levels of thought the reader can see easily. For example, imagine the central idea for a document is "three changes in the billing system." That central idea might have three main points, one for each change in the billing system:

1.   Improving the dunning letters

2.   Using a new invoice form

3.   Beginning a new method of tracking payments

The three main points are called Level 1 points because they are at the highest level; they explain the central idea.

Follow this procedure to write the key term for each Level 1 point that explains the central idea. If the document has more than one central idea, repeat this process for each central idea. Write as many words as you need to identify the point explicitly, but no more. Resist writing sentences you feel you need to edit.

1. Skip a line under the central point key term and write a word or a few words describing the first Level 1 point the reader will need to understand to accomplish your business objectives. These words comprise the first Level 1 point key term.

2. Below that first Level 1 point key term, write key terms for the other Level 1 points you know the reader must understand, placing each one on its own line.

3. Place a number 1 before each Level 1 point key term. Every Level 1 point must be separate from every other. In other words, you shouldn't have a Level 1 point that explains another Level 1 point.

Critical tests:

After you have written the Level 1 point key terms, evaluate them by answering these critical questions:

1. **Will these Level 1 points provide all the information this reader needs?** Look at your evaluations for knowledge of the subject, education, technical knowledge, need for concreteness, and need for depth. Add any information you believe this reader will need.

2. **Do I have any Level 1 points this reader does not need?** Delete any unnecessary points. Include only the information that is necessary to achieve your objectives.

❖ Example

These are the notes for a document using the illustration of levels presented in the previous example. The writer has chosen not to capitalize the Level 1 point key terms.

THREE CHANGES IN THE BILLING SYSTEM

1 improving dunning letters

1 using new invoice forms

1 using a new method for tracking payments

Write key terms for the sub-points explaining the main points.

Each Level 1 point will have sub-points explaining it. A sub-point that explains a Level 1 point is a Level 2 point. Below each Level 1 point key term, write key terms for Level 2 points that explain it. You may go back and forth between the Level 1 points, adding Level 2 points as they come to you. Allow yourself to think freely so you consider everything you must explain in the document.

Evaluate the Level 2 points as you did the Level 1 points. Do you have what this reader needs, considering the reader's knowledge of the subject, education, technical knowledge, need for concreteness, and need for depth? If not, add it.

Is any information unnecessary? If so, delete it.

Write key terms for the remaining levels to the depth the reader needs.

If a Level 2 point has information explaining it, the points in that information are Level 3 points. Continue adding levels to the depth the reader needs. Write numbers to show the levels.

Evaluate the points as you did the Level 1 and Level 2 points. Do you have what this reader needs, considering the reader's knowledge of the subject, education, technical knowledge, need for concreteness, and need for depth? If not, add it. Is any information unnecessary? If so, delete it.

❖ Example

These are the notes someone might write for the report about the three changes in billing procedures referred to in a previous example. The numbers to the left of the key terms show the levels. The writer has capitalized the Level 1 key terms to keep them separate from lower level key terms.

This writer has chosen to put the key terms into longer phrases, with some forming sentences. However, she has resisted trying to edit them to make them perfect sentences.

The important parts of the key terms are the words that represent concepts, such as "improve dunning letters" and "opportunities to pay over time." Words such as "offering," "by which," and "with" just make the meaning of the key terms clear for the writer as she prepares her notes. When she writes later, she will keep the important words in the key term words and drop or change the unimportant words.

THREE CHANGES IN THE BILLING SYSTEM

1 IMPROVING DUNNING LETTERS
    2 Offering opportunities to pay over time
    2 Extending the time by which payments must be made
    2 Listing a local collection agency with a local address
        3 Customers respond better to local agencies
        3 We identified local agencies in twenty cities
        3 Their names will appear on dunning letters

1 USING NEW INVOICE FORMS
    2 Explaining the taxes more clearly
    2 Including our telephone payment number

1 USING A NEW METHOD FOR TRACKING PAYMENTS

If this report were intended to provide general information for all employees in the Billing Department, the three levels of detail in the report likely would provide the depth of information most employees needed. However, for the Billing Department employees who will have to carry out these changes, the writer may need to add depth with Level 4, Level 5, and even Level 6 details. For example, these employees would need to know the names and addresses of the local agencies, how the names will appear on the letters, how to coordinate with the agencies, and so on.

For documents that have a format, such as an audit report, write the major headings for the report and then work with sections one at a time.

Documents such as audit reports have fairly prescribed formats. Treat each section as a central idea. Write the heading you must use for each section in caps. Below each, write notes for the Level 1 points within the section. Then write notes for the Level 2 points explaining the Level 1 points. Finish by writing notes for points at any deeper levels.

Write the points in order so you can ensure that the points in earlier sections have counterparts in later sections. Every section of a report such as an audit report should have points that correspond to the points in the other sections. Write the key terms for all of the sections of the report before beginning to write the detail. That will enable you to organize the report and ensure that you follow through with the points in each section.

❖ Example

The first three required sections for a company's audit report might be INTRODUCTION, PURPOSE, and SCOPE. The notes might look like this:

INTRODUCTION
1 audit grant expenditures
  2 conduct annually

1 granting agency requirements
  2 record expenditures and remaining money
  2 submit to their accounting firm

PURPOSE
1 provide accounting of expenditures and remaining money
1 anticipate additional needs

SCOPE
1 only expenditures from granting agency money
1 not expenditures from internal matching funds

For instructions and procedures, write key terms for every critical action.

Instructions and procedures are difficult to follow when they don't include all of the steps the reader must complete with sufficient detail for the reader to be successful. Identify every action the reader must perform and write a key term for each in your notes. Be sure you have not omitted actions and that you have written in sufficient detail for this reader to be successful. If the reader has insufficient detail at any step in the process, the procedure will break down at that step.

In your notes, specify every resource the reader will need to have to be successful. For example, the resources may be forms, contact people, Web pages, or computer screens.

Revise the words to make them precise
key terms appropriate for the readers.

After you have written the key terms in levels to the depth you need for each reader, decide whether the words you've used are the most precise, accurate key terms for the concepts. You will use these key terms throughout the document, so change them as necessary to make them precise and accurate.

Judge whether the key terms fit the knowledge and technical expertise evaluations you made for this reader. If you have given the reader a knowledge evaluation of "low knowledge" or technical expertise evaluation of "low technical expertise," use the plain English alternatives rather than specialized jargon, unless you believe you need to teach the reader the specialized terms. If you have rated this person's knowledge as "high knowledge" or technical expertise as "high technical expertise," use the jargon terms. If you are in doubt, use the plain words.

Best Practice

Respond to requests by providing precisely what the person asked for, under the conditions specified.

Guidelines for this best practice:

1. Identify the requester's expectations in the key terms.

2. Write the notes for your response below the person's key terms.

3. Use questions in the request as your guide to select information and write the response.

4. If the reader needs to solve a problem or deal with a situation, use the problem or situation key terms in the request as your guide.

5. If you aren't clear about what the requester wants, clarify it.

6. Respond to all e-mail messages promptly.

Your document responding to a request must provide everything the requester wants, under the conditions the requester requires. You may be responding to a request you receive in an e-mail, writing a proposal in response to an RFP (request for proposal), or completing a standard activity the company or agency requires periodically, such as a periodic audit. In these cases, the readers require a response that satisfies their expectations and is delivered under the conditions they specify.

Identify the requester's expectations in the key terms.

When you receive the person's request, identify the key terms in the request that specify this person's expectations:

1. **WHAT** the reader wants from you

2. **CONDITIONS** the reader expects you to adhere to

Record the key terms the requester wrote, in the order in which the requester wrote them. Write them in a column using a new line for each request key term.

❖ Example

You receive this request in an e-mail:

> Give me a brief report on how the attendance has been at the trainings you've done since August. I need to know especially whether the salespeople have been able to make it to the sessions. Get it to me by Friday afternoon.

Write the key terms the requester used to describe what she **WANTS** at the beginning of your document and assign each to be a Level 1 topic.

  1 - how the attendance has been at the trainings since August

  1 - whether salespeople have been to the sessions

Write the requester's **CONDITION** key terms with a blank line between each:

  brief

  by Friday afternoon

When you write your response, include the requester's key terms for what she wants, exactly as they appear in the request. That ensures that you are providing everything the requester asked for because her words guide your response. This is the introduction to the report responding to the request:

This report explains the following:

   1. How the attendance has been at the trainings we've done since August

   2. Whether the salespeople have been able to make it to the sessions

1. **How the attendance has been at the trainings we've done since August**

   We have had 92 percent of all employees attending the trainings we've done since August. [The report continues here.]

After you have written the report, reexamine the condition key terms that are on the first page to be sure you are satisfying the requester's conditions. Then delete them for the final draft.

Write the notes for your response below the person's request key terms.

Each of the person's request key terms is a heading for your response. Below the heading, write the key terms for a complete response that provides everything the person asked for, to the level of detail the person needs. Number the key terms to show the levels.

Critical tests:

Evaluate the information by answering these critical questions:

1. **Have I provided all the information this reader requested and needs?** Consider this person's knowledge of the subject, education, technical knowledge, need for concreteness, and need for depth. Add any information this reader expects or needs.

2. **Do I have any information this reader has not requested or does not need?** Delete any unnecessary information. Include only the information the person asked for and needs.

Use questions in the request as your guide.

If you are answering questions contained in an e-mail, RFP, audit guidelines, or other source of questions, use the words in the questions or guidelines for the request key terms. Usually, begin your response by repeating the question or guideline. If you do not repeat the entire question or guideline, at least repeat the key term.

❖ Example

The writer receives this request:

> Frieda, I'm finishing the final report on the project and have some questions. How many hours were spent completing the project design? Did you include travel costs in the final costs? I think we were below budget. Is that true?
> Jim

The first question in the request is, "How many hours were spent completing the project design?" The request key term is "hours spent completing the project design."

In the following response, the writer includes the question, verbatim, and uses the key term in the response. The bolding would be in an e-mail if the e-mail supported it:

> Hello Jim,
>
> You asked how many hours we spent completing the project design, whether I included travel costs in the final costs, and whether we were below budget. My answers follow.
>
> **Question 1:** How many hours were spent completing the project design?
>
> **Answer:** We spent 74 hours completing the project design.

The requester's first question appears exactly as it was in the request. The key term from the question is in the opening, the question, and the answer. In explicit business writing, you must be so clear you cannot be misunderstood, so you write in ways that look and feel different from the old business writing that grew out of journalism and creative writing. *It looks different, but to be consistently explicit, business writing must look this way.*

If the reader needs to solve a problem or deal with a situation, use the problem or situation key terms in the request as your guide.

If you must respond to a problem or situation the requester describes, write the requester's problem or situation key terms on the first page before you respond. When you write, restate the problem or situation using the key terms. Before you send the document, reexamine the key terms to make sure you've responded to the problem or situation.

❖ Example

This is the request the business writer receives. The problem key terms are bolded just for this illustration:

Hello Eric,

I need some help with the program. I was on the **house description screen** putting in the **information for the client's house** and it asked for **number of baths** and it didn't work. The program **wouldn't save** it. I **put in 2.5 baths** and it kept **changing it to 3 baths.**

Lisa

In your response, summarize the problem before explaining the solution. That lets the reader know you understand the problem, and it helps you provide a solution for the real problem.

This is the writer's response to the e-mail.

Hello Lisa,

I'll help you with the problem. You wrote that you were on **the house description screen** putting in the **information for the client's house.** You put in **2.5 baths** and **saved** it. Then, when you looked at the "Baths" field, it contained **3 baths,** not **2.5 baths.**

The problem is that the program . . . [continues here]

In the best practices that create clear business writing, the writer must ensure that the reader understands the context and the content of the writing. State the problem at the beginning so the reader can respond if you misunderstood. Frustrating miscommunication can occur when the writer provides an answer to a problem that doesn't exist. More damage sometimes results when the reader tries to apply the wrong solution and it makes the real problem worse.

Describing the problem at the beginning also reminds the reader about the issue that prompted your response. The reader may have forgotten the detail.

There is another benefit to both you and the reader when you explain the issue at the beginning of the document. Writing the explanation takes you only a few seconds because you're focusing on it at the time. However, you may save the reader a few minutes of having to locate and read the request to remember what was in it. When others consistently write the background of documents they send to you, they will save you the few minutes it would take you to remember that you're receiving a document responding to a request you've forgotten.

If you aren't clear about what the requester wants, clarify it.

If you aren't clear about what the requester wants, contact the requester to find out. Don't guess. Mistaken guesses frustrate requesters, result in back-and-forth e-mail messages that clog in-boxes, and waste your time in rewriting. Your request for clarification also lets the writer know the message wasn't explicit. Writers need to hear from readers about their writing. Hopefully, in a corporate climate that rewards and expects quality writing, the writer will make an effort to be clearer next time.

Respond to all e-mail messages promptly.

One of the conditions you should satisfy for all e-mail, whether the writer specifies it or not, is responding promptly. We should respond to e-mail as we do to phone calls, not as we do to letters.

1. Always respond to e-mail messages within an hour or two of receiving them when you are in the office, but no later than four hours. If you are out, have someone respond for you, or create an autoresponder explaining that you're out for the day and when you will respond.

2. Leave no e-mail message unanswered at the end of the business day when possible, but certainly not by the end of the morning

the next day. At least respond to say you will need more time to respond and will do so in a few hours or the next day.

3. Respond to every e-mail message. Never put a message into the "later" pile that is really a trash can.

Best Practice

Give readers the information they need at the specific points where they need it for maximum understanding.

Guidelines for this best practice:

1. Organize the Level 1 points first.

2. Organize the Level 2 points next.

3. Organize the remaining points at all other levels.

4. For instructions and procedures, organize the key terms so readers have what they need at the precise point at which they need it.

5. End by reviewing the organization from the first page to the last.

Organize the notes you have written so they present information the readers need, when they need it. The procedure that follows will seem time consuming because you must concentrate and proceed slowly as you learn it. However, when you become adept at following these steps through practice, you will perform them quickly and easily. Like the other best practices in this book, they will become second nature to you.

Organize the Level 1 points first.

Organize the Level 1 point key terms explaining the central idea according to what the reader needs to be able to understand the central idea. Don't work with the Level 2 points until you have finished organizing the Level 1 points. Don't write sentences yet.

If you have two or more central ideas, decide which central idea the reader needs first and put it first in the document. Then organize the Level 1 points for that central idea. After you finish organizing the Level 1 points for the first central idea, organize the Level 1 points for the other central ideas.

Organize the Level 2 points next.

Then organize the Level 2 points listed under the Level 1 points until you have organized all Level 2 points for a central idea. That way, you will see the organization of the entire document at a Level 2 depth before going into deeper levels. It is as though you were viewing a summary of the document so you can evaluate whether the information is sufficient, necessary, and organized.

You will also be able to see whether you have written some Level 2 points twice. That will be a signal to rethink the Level 1 points. You may decide you should combine two Level 1 points because you're repeating Level 2 points in them.

Organize the remaining points at all other levels.

Then go on to the Level 3 points in the same way. Focus on the Level 3 points throughout the explanation of the central idea before going on to Level 4 points. Continue this process until you have finished all the points whose key terms you have listed.

For instructions and procedures, organize the key terms so readers have what they need at the precise point at which they need it.

For instructions and procedures, organize the key terms so all the information readers need to make a decision or perform an action is at the point at which the reader makes the decision or performs the action. Don't explain information at one point and expect the reader to remember it and use it to make a decision at a later point.

Don't refer the reader to another place in the document to read information necessary for deciding or acting at the current place.

End by reviewing the organization from the first page to the last.

Finally, read the key terms from beginning to end to see whether this organization of the document will help the reader follow the thoughts and understand the points well enough to achieve your objectives.

Best Practice

When readers have differing needs or abilities, write different versions of the document or sections within the document to match the readers' needs and abilities.

Guidelines for this best practice:

Option 1: Write separate documents for readers with differing needs or abilities.

Option 2: Write different parts for readers with differing needs or abilities.

Option 3: Use sidebars, boxed text, and other devices to include different explanations on the same pages for readers with differing needs or abilities.

Often, business writers must write a document for several readers with different needs or abilities. For example, readers of an audit report may include the auditor's manager, the client's manager, the client's upper-level executives, and the technical specialists who must act on the audit. These different readers have different technical backgrounds and differing needs for explanation, concreteness, and depth.

Explicit business writing uses strategies that address the needs and abilities of every reader. If a team of business writers must write regularly for the same readers, the team should develop strategies together and evaluate their success together.

Decide on a method of presenting the information before you organize the key terms you have in the notes. The method will determine in part how you organize the document.

Three options for presenting text suitable to readers' differing needs and abilities follow.

Option 1:   Write separate documents for readers with differing needs or abilities.

The most desirable option is to write a different e-mail, memo, letter, or report for each group of readers. Writing different documents to fit their different needs or abilities provides dividends in reader understanding that make it worth the effort.

Business people sometimes write one e-mail to several people with comments addressed to each. If you are writing an e-mail to several people who have different needs and messages, consider whether every reader will benefit from reading the messages intended for the others. If not, write separate e-mails with individualized messages.

Option 2:   Write different parts for readers with differing needs or abilities.

A second option when you write for readers with different needs and abilities is to write different parts for different readers. For example, you might write a non-technical executive summary at the beginning of a technical report for the readers who just want the summary and have low technical expertise. If the non-technical reader needs more depth, you might write a non-technical report and put technical information in appendixes, referenced in the non-technical explanations.

Decide on the sections of the report based on your readers' needs, not a format for reports that someone developed in the past. The traditional section you might use for the non-technical explanation is the executive summary. However, you could instead create two large sections titled "Non-technical Report" and "Technical Detail Report," with the non-technical report referencing the technical report. Any division of the report is appropriate if it satisfies the needs of all the readers.

Option 3: Use devices to include different explanations on a page for readers with differing needs or abilities.

A third option is to use boxed text, split pages, sidebars, or other devices to include explanations for different readers on the same pages. For example, you might put the technical or non-technical explanation in a box on the page, with the remainder of the page devoted to the alternative level of technical explanation.

NEXRAD's sensitivity depends on the pulse mode. The beam is in a series of pulses emitted for a specified duration. The time from the start of one pulse to the start of the next is the pulse repetition time.

When NEXRAD is transmitting in short-pulse mode, the pulse duration is 1.57 microseconds and the wavelength is 300,000km by 0.00000157 seconds for a length of 471 meters. The radar then stops transmitting and waits 998.43 micro-seconds for an echo from the transmitted beam. The pulse duration of 1.57 micro-seconds plus the listening period of 998.43 micro-seconds form the pulse-repetition time of 1000 microseconds, which is the same as 1 millisecond, or 1/1000th of a second. Since the radar is sending out a pulse every 1/1000th of a second, it is sending out 1000 pulses per second.

When NEXRAD is transmitting in long-pulse mode, the pulse duration is extended to 4.7 microseconds for a wavelength of 1410 meters. The longer the pulse, the greater the amount of energy scattered by a target and the greater the amount of energy that will be received by the radar.

Thus, NEXRAD is more sensitive when operating in long-pulse mode.

Summary

The amount of detail NEXRAD shows depends on the pulse mode. In a short-pulse mode, NEXRAD sends out a radar beam for a brief time (as short as 1.57 millionths of a second), then listens for the echo for 998.43 millionths of a second.

In a long-pulse mode, NEXRAD sends out a radar beam for 4.7 millionths of a second, then listens for the echo for 998.43 millionths of a second.

Because the long-pulse mode sends out more radar energy, the echo NEXRAD receives is stronger, so NEXRAD shows more detail when operating in the long-pulse mode.

Best Practice

Present topics in the same order throughout and link all the contents in each part.

If the document begins with a list of issues, recommendations, conclusions, or similar subjects explained in the document, you must use the item key terms and same order of the items throughout.

Similarly, some business documents have sections whose contents must correspond to each other. For example, a report about an evaluation study may have objectives, evaluation criteria, results, and recommendations. The contents of these sections must correspond to each other precisely. Sometimes, business writers mistakenly treat these sections as independent of one another, so an objective may not have a corresponding evaluation method, or a recommendation may be unrelated to any of the results. Each section must correspond to the preceding and succeeding sections.

❖ Example

Imagine you are writing a report containing sections for objectives, evaluation criteria, results, and recommendations. The first section has four objectives. The rest of the report must follow the pattern set in the four objectives:

1. The second section is "Evaluation Criteria." Each evaluation criterion must correspond to one of the four objectives, and the evaluation criteria must appear in the same order as the objectives.

2. The next section is "Results." The results must correspond to the four objectives and evaluation criteria and must appear in the same order. If unexpected results occur, you should present them following the explanations of the results that fit with the evaluation criteria and objectives.

3. The last section is "Recommendations." Each recommendation must correspond to an objective, an evaluation criterion, and a result, and you should present them in the same order you used in the preceding sections.

❖ Example

In this poorly written example, the writer has described three issues and recommendations to address the issues. The document should have two parts: issues and recommendations. However, the document does not clearly explain the issues or relate the issues to the recommendations.

> I am concerned with some issues regarding the certification tests taken by new employees. Nearly 30 percent of participants are failing the tests; many participants stated that they do not have enough time to study the required material; participants remark that the contents sometimes do not match what they end up doing on the job; and more than 20 percent of scheduled participants do not show up.
>
> I recommend we reconstruct the material on the tests. Our department would observe employees doing work tasks and solicit information from your staff to include in the tests. That will give us a clearer understanding of what material to include or exclude on the new tests.
>
> Also, the certification tests should be given six weeks after on-the-job experience and classroom attendance for each employee. This would allow sufficient time for employees to study and revisit problem areas that they have encountered during that time. The process will involve having the employees document their questions and provide them to their branch trainers, who will help them prepare for the tests.
>
> In addition, I propose that we send reminder e-mails two weeks and two days prior to the test. Management will also need to stress the importance of the certification tests to new employees during their introductory period and explain that dismissal can occur if they do not take the test by a certain time.

To make the explanation explicit, the writer should have used the key terms, "issues" and "recommendations," consistently and followed the same organization in the recommendations as in the issues. The key terms in the issues should appear in the recommendations. An example of how it could be written more explicitly follows.

Below are four issues with the certification tests taken by new employees. My recommendations follow the list of issues.

ISSUES

1. Nearly 30 percent of participants are failing the tests.

2. Many participants state that they do not have enough time to study the required material.

3. Participants remark that the contents sometimes do not match what they end up doing on the job.

4. More than 20 percent of scheduled participants do not show up.

RECOMMENDATIONS

Issues 1 and 2   Nearly 30 percent of participants are failing the tests, and many state that they do not have enough time to study the required material.

Recommendation

We should administer the certification tests six weeks after on-the-job experience and classroom attendance for each employee. This would allow sufficient time for employees to study and revisit problem areas that they have encountered during that time. Employees would provide their questions to their branch trainers, who would help them prepare for the tests.

Issue 3   Participants remark that contents sometimes do not match what they end up doing on the job.

Recommendation

We recommend reconstructing the material on the tests to match what they do on the job. Our department would observe employees doing work tasks and solicit information from your staff to include in the tests. That would give us a clearer understanding of what material to include and exclude on the new tests.

| Issue 4 | More than 20 percent of scheduled participants do not show up. |

Recommendation

To eliminate the problem of scheduled participants failing to show up, we can send reminder e-mails two weeks prior to the test and again two days prior to the test. Management will also need to stress the importance of the certification tests to new employees during their introductory period and explain that they could be dismissed if they do not take the test by a certain time.

Explicit business writing uses patterns to make the information easier to follow and understand. Use the same patterns throughout the document. At all times, when you list the issues, conclusions, recommendations, or other items in one place, follow the same order when you refer to them in any other place. Identify them explicitly using the same key terms so the reader can see them clearly.

Chapter 5

Explicit business writing that achieves objectives fosters a climate of cooperation and an expectation for quality in written communication.

Successful business writing achieves the writer's objectives. However, readers may not cooperate in achieving the objectives if they commonly receive antagonistic, confrontational, distant messages from the writer. Messages will more likely be successful if the writers and readers feel they are on the same team, as partners working together to be successful. As a result, business writers should write cooperatively and cordially.

The corporate climate must also show that the company and employees value quality communication. Explicit writing should be rewarded; unclear, careless writing should be corrected. Managers and employees must show that they value successful written communication by freely giving and receiving comments about writing, and they should actively work to improve their writing based on the comments. Written communication that consistently achieves business objectives requires a climate in which everyone in the company or agency expects quality writing in every document and provides the feedback writers need to improve their writing and be rewarded for quality writing.

The best practices in this chapter develop a corporate culture that
- builds successful, cooperative teams through writing
- rewards quality writing
- encourages growth in writing competence

Best Practice

In e-mails, letters, and memos, write thanks, commendations, and genuine statements of good will that build teams and partnerships with clients.

Some business people contact The Business Writing Center saying that they want to learn the techniques of writing an e-mail, letter, or memo so readers don't view it as being curt, unfriendly, or harsh. We explain that they misunderstand what makes a message seem unfriendly or harsh to the reader. The way the reader perceives the message in the current e-mail depends on the relationship the writer has developed with the reader over past e-mails.

To have your co-workers feel your writing is cordial, and to have your client feel you are being cooperative and partnering, you must set the tone over weeks and months of correspondence, not simply in one e-mail, memo, or letter. If you've been harsh, patronizing, insensitive, and distant in previous e-mails, today's e-mail will have little effect on the tone you've already established. No magic writing technique will gain the reader's cooperation if you haven't built a cooperative relationship before now.

To cultivate the cooperation you want in the future, look for opportunities to build the team or client relationship every time you write an e-mail, letter, or memo. Congratulate, say thanks, and give praise as often as you can genuinely do so. Every message is an opportunity to build a team spirit with others in your company and a partnering relationship with vendors and clients. These are examples of statements someone might write:

> You've always been knowledgeable about this client. I need your help.

> Thanks for sending that report so quickly.

> I'm looking forward to hearing more of your good ideas at this meeting.

Some business people have the feeling that making statements like these seems fake or insincere. Readers don't see it that way when someone writes those words to them. We're all pleased by such comments. Of course, the message should always be genuine, and if you begin every e-mail, letter, or memo with such a message, soon people are going to stop reading the first sentences of anything you send.   Write a cordial greeting only when you mean it, but look for opportunities to write one, and anticipate that if you never write such messages, you may have difficulty convincing people in today's message that you really regard them as competent, valued colleagues.

Best Practice

Present the information with consideration for the reader's possible reaction to the subject and to you.

To achieve your business objectives, you must have the reader's cooperation. Before you begin the e-mail, letter, or memo message, ask yourself, "Will the reader react negatively to anything in this message?" If so, defuse the reaction by beginning with a buffer to reassure the reader as much as is appropriate.

People always assume the worst. If you write something negative, even if you do it with an attitude of good will, the reader may not sense your positive thoughts and feelings. Instead, the worst possible interpretation will likely color anything you say, regardless of what it is. However, there is always something positive in every situation. Don't minimize or dilute a message the reader must hear, even though it may not be good news. However, make a point of writing that positive statement before you give the reader the bad news.

❖ Example

The following e-mail contains an important message, but the writer presents it without a buffer, so it sounds harsh:

> Jackson,
>
> In the most recent batch, your data had three errors. You have to eliminate the errors or we'll have to transfer you out of the department into a job where you don't work with details.
>
> Doris

This is the same message with a buffer that states Doris's genuine thoughts about the situation. Jackson needs to know the consequences, but Doris begins with some words of encouragement. She reiterates the encouragement at the end.

> Jackson,
>
> I really appreciate your effort to reduce the number of errors you have in your work. I'm going to make myself available this week to help you try to reduce them to zero.
>
> In the most recent batch, your data had three errors. You have to eliminate the errors or we'll have to transfer you out of the department into a job where you don't work with details.
>
> Let's work together on it. I'm sure you'll eliminate the errors this week.
>
> Doris

The message is still there, word for word, and the consequences are no less severe. However, the encouragement at the beginning sets a tone for the entire message.

The buffer must appear at the beginning. You will paint the entire message with the color you use at the beginning, regardless of the words that come later. Here is the same message with the paragraphs reversed so the buffer is at the end. The buffer loses some of its positive impact.

> Jackson,
>
> In the most recent batch, your data had three errors. You have to eliminate the errors or we'll have to transfer you out of the department into a job where you don't work with details.
>
> I really appreciate your effort to reduce the number of errors you have in your work. I'm going to make myself available this week to help you try to reduce them to zero.
>
> Doris

Put the buffer first to help the reader see the positive perspective you have about it. Repeat the buffer at the end to have maximum impact.

Best Practice

Use the tone and level of formality that fit the objectives and the reader.

> **Guidelines for this best practice:**
> 1. Choose a tone that builds a partnership.
> 2. Use the level of formality appropriate for the content and reader.
> 3. Use formal style for the business parts of e-mails.

An e-mail, memo, letter, or report conveys more than information; it gives the reader a sense of how the writer feels about herself, the reader, the company, and the subject. Explicit business writing builds on a history of successful past interactions so today's e-mail, memo, letter, or report will more likely result in achieving the writer's business objectives.

Choose a tone that builds a partnership.

The tone the writer uses contributes to developing a history of interactions that will result in future communication successes or future obstruction and failure.

Three examples of tones that create negative histories of interaction follow. A fourth example then uses a helpful, positive tone to create a positive history. Notice that the information is the same in each example, but the tones differ markedly.

Tone of disregard for the readers

In the example that follows, the writer has little regard for the readers. The writer's tone suggests that the readers should already know the information, and this report is a waste of the writer's time. The statements will alienate the readers and make future collaboration more difficult. The message written to employees from the department manager explains the need to come to meetings prepared to participate.

> Employees of Atkinson Company should know by now that they have important responsibilities in preparing for meetings and in the meetings themselves. However, some employees apparently are not as knowledgeable about them as they should be, judging from recent performance. Therefore, I have compiled a report listing and explaining these responsibilities.
>
> Your management expects all employees to study this report in depth immediately, or they may be publicly embarrassed during the upcoming meeting due to not knowing the contents when asked about them.

Impersonal tone

The tone can also be impersonal. It isn't harsh; it just lets the reader know that in this company, everyone is a cog in the wheel. If the reader leaves, the company will just hire another cog. This is a letter to employees the manager meets in the hall every day.

> Employees of Atkinson Company should know their responsibilities in preparing for meetings and in the meetings themselves. Please study this report in depth immediately. Your conscientious attention to this matter is appreciated.

Patronizing tone

Writers may fall into a patronizing tone when they're trying to encourage readers. The underlying message is that the writer is the missionary and the reader is an unwashed heathen. Avoid the patronizing tone; don't insinuate that the reader is unschooled, careless, immature, or stupid.

You have important responsibilities in preparing for meetings and in the meetings themselves. Business people have to take the reins of their lives and their positions in the company. You can't let others do it for you. You have to pull your weight. Keep saying "I'm on the team and I can do this." Then pitch in and give it all you've got.

I've prepared a report on what you can do to prepare for and participate in meetings. Take it seriously and you'll get where you want to go in the company. Let's hear from everyone at the next meeting— you can do it!

Helpful tone

This is the same message with a more helpful tone. It shows a regard for the readers that will encourage them to read and use the information. Future collaborations will be congenial and productive.

Notice the underlying messages: "I have confidence in you," "I regard you as a conscientious professional," "I value your participation," "I look forward to your comments at the next meeting." These messages are all in the tone of the message.

Your feedback and suggestions are important for our department's continued success. The comments you give during meetings have been especially useful to me. As a result, I have prepared a description of the ways in which we can all prepare for and participate in meetings to maintain and enhance the discussions.

If you have not been sharing your thoughts in meetings, make this your opportunity to begin doing so. Your comments and suggestions are valuable to the department.

We will talk about the contents of this report at the next meeting so you can share your reactions to it and your suggestions for making it a useful document that will help us all prepare for and participate in meetings. Come with your insights so we can hear from everyone.

The manager can expect congenial, cooperative responses to the next e-mail, memo, letter, or report he sends to the employees. The success of the next document will depend in part on the attitude resulting from this correspondence.

However, if the manager sending this message has been manipulative in the past, showing little regard for employees in correspondence, even this congenial message will be viewed with suspicion. The attitude with which readers receive a message will depend in large part upon the relationship the writer has established with the readers over many past messages.

Choose a level of formality appropriate for the content and reader.

Formal style: all business

The **formal style** contains no casual or conversational statements. It is all business. Use the formal style when you are presenting information, procedures, findings, recommendations, and any other factual, straightforward information. Using a formal style doesn't mean using complex words and long sentences, however. It just means that you don't present the message casually. This letter uses a formal style:

Dear Jason,

Attached is a brief report that explains what Jackson Consulting Services needs from you to be able to analyze Talidon Financial Systems' financial position and prospects.

We also need access to the financial records data. However, if you aren't able to access the data easily, we will use other data or compile the information ourselves.

Sincerely,

Sondra Lester
Account Manager

Informal style: cordial, casual, and personal

An **informal style** is more cordial, casual, and personal. However, it should not contain slang, incomplete sentences, emotional statements, inappropriate humor, or statements unacceptable for a business setting.

Sometimes, you may use an informal style for the entire document, such as a letter of congratulations or a persuasive e-mail. For most other business writing, however, reserve the informal style for the parts of the document that convey your cordial, partnering relationship with the reader. Write the text that will achieve your business objectives using a formal style.

This rewritten version of the previous example has an informal opening, a brief note of empathy in the middle, and a cordial closing. The rest, however, is all business, using a formal style. The informal parts are bolded for this illustration.

Dear Jason,

Thanks for the wonderful hospitality during my visit. You were right; I really liked the French cuisine. I bought a cookbook as soon as I got home.

Attached is a brief report that explains what Jackson Consulting Services needs from you to be able to analyze Talidon Financial Systems' financial position and prospects.

We also need access to the financial records data. **I understand the problem you've had with the data archives.** If you aren't able to access the data easily, we will use other data or compile the information ourselves.

I look forward to a long and mutually beneficial relationship with Talidon. Call me if you have any questions.

Sincerely,

Sondra Lester
Account Manager

Use a formal style for the business parts of e-mails.

E-mail began as a conversational medium for online chats before becoming the primary medium for business communication. As a result, some business people write e-mail using a style that is so informal it sounds flippant. However, as the primary mode of communicating in business today, the business parts of e-mail must be all business all the time; they must be formal, concise, and objective.

Business writers should feel free to begin e-mails with a cordial, conversational greeting. Then, to communicate explicitly, the information parts of the e-mail should be straightforward, concise, and objective.

This is an example of a conversational e-mail:

Hi Barry,

 Brian phoned me and he's sure Lester and Frieda are getting together on the vendor thing. He talked to Bonnie today and she is floored about their suggestion of using Office Center when Barton's is closer and cheaper, from the bid information.....Lester-Frieda's link to Baxter at OC is pretty clear....don't know how they're figuring we can't see that??? Anyway, closer/cheaper has got it all the way!!!! Besides, mgt's on this thing about getting bids and this would fit requirements to a T. Let's just say what's the point....Barton's is closer and cheaper. Just memo it.

Lena

These are the problems with this casual style:

1. Rumors and personal or emotional statements are not appropriate for business writing. Barry and Lena might exchange thoughts over coffee at lunch, but they should not write them in business e-mails.

2. The shorthand, conversational style doesn't communicate clearly and may lead to misunderstanding.

3. This style adds words to the message without focusing on the core points. The reader must spend more time reading than is warranted.

4. The style leads to improper grammar and punctuation, increasing the likelihood that the message will be misunderstood.

The writer should begin with a cordial greeting, then shift into a formal style, stating the issue and action explicitly, as in the following example:

Hi Barry,

I received your e-mail about the problems with choosing a vendor. I understand your frustration with the process. Thanks for working at it in spite of the obstacles.

Lester and Frieda have recommended that we use Office Center for our new vendor. However, the bids we received showed that Barton's is cheaper, and we are now required to award contracts based on the bids. As a result, we must choose Barton's. Draft a memo explaining that to everyone in the department.

Let's get together for lunch tomorrow if you have time. We can talk about what has been going on then.

Lena

The business content that was in the first example is still in this rewritten version. However, the innuendo and unnecessary comments have been omitted. The sentences are clear, well written, and straightforward. Lena offers to have a more casual conversation about what has happened over lunch. That is the appropriate time for it, and Barry knows Lena is reserving her more personal comments for their lunch together because that is the standard that has been set in the company. As a result, Barry doesn't feel that Lena is ignoring what they both know to be true about the situation—it's just that an e-mail isn't the place to communicate it.

Best Practice

Ask for and give feedback on the clarity and relevance of documents and writing.

Guidelines for this best practice:

1. Ask for feedback about the clarity of your writing.

2. Give writers feedback about the clarity of their writing.

3. Give writers feedback about the relevance of the content in their documents.

When you give feedback about someone else's writing and ask for comments on your own writing, you help build a corporate culture in which everyone expects high quality writing and helps others improve their writing. You will benefit by becoming a more capable writer, and you will encourage the quality communication from others that will give you what you need to be able to act quickly and successfully. Everyone wins.

Ask for feedback about the clarity of your writing.

Find out from readers how well your writing communicates and whether it satisfies their needs. Adjust your future documents to make them even clearer and more relevant for readers. Over time, your writing will become increasingly effective with these readers.

❖ Examples

Let me know whether this explanation is clear for you.

I thought your comments about Jim's proposal were very clear and well organized. When you respond, tell me whether my explanations in this e-mail are OK. I'd like to keep mine at that quality level.

I worked at writing this summary so it wouldn't be unnecessarily technical. Call me after you read this to let me know if I was successful.

Give writers feedback about the clarity of their writing.

Take every opportunity to give praise for clear documents and express your appreciation to writers who take a few extra minutes to write clearly. If the document is unclear or incomplete, explain that to the writer by using "I" words without judgment or blame. Describe your difficulty in understanding rather than the writer's inability to write. Write, "I couldn't grasp what you were writing in the last paragraph" rather than "Your writing in the last paragraph was really bad."

❖ Examples

> I needed more information about the machine to be able to operate it. More concrete explanations will help me perform correctly.
>
> I found myself getting distracted by the spelling errors and lack of capitalization so I had to read the e-mail several times. Let me know if I misunderstood your message.

At the same time, if the company has a clear set of standards for writing, such as those in Chapters 13 to 16, you can point out to writers the standards they are not following. That will be much easier if the company, at all levels, has established the expectation that all employees follow the standards because of the resulting clear writing that benefits everyone.

Give writers feedback about the relevance of the content in their documents.

Let writers know whether their responses to you were precisely what you wanted and no more. If they include irrelevant information, let them know that. The only way to ensure that you receive what you want and no more is to let the writers know whether they're sending what you want and need. If you don't tell them that you would prefer not to receive unnecessary information when they send it, and you don't tell them when you are pleased with a document that provides precisely what you want, they will not learn what you expect from them.

Receiving the response you want today depends upon the feedback you've provided to them about their previous responses to your requests.

For e-mail messages, let writers know whether the content of their e-mail is useful to you. E-mail inboxes become clogged with unnecessary e-mail messages. Readers learn that the information in some writers' e-mails is often irrelevant, so they may

- simply ignore the messages, resulting in the frustrated writer sending more e-mails trying to elicit a response, or

- skim the e-mail and respond without explaining to the writer that they would prefer not to receive that kind of information.

When the reader doesn't explain that the information is irrelevant, the writer doesn't learn to adjust the messages to provide only relevant information, so the reader can expect to receive more of the same types of messages in the future.

Important messages also become lost in the sea of words. When e-mail from someone often contains superfluous information, readers learn not to read her messages. When she really needs something, she doesn't get the response she wants, even though she feels she wrote it in plain English. Readers have learned to ignore or skim her messages.

E-mail will become an efficient medium for business communication if the corporate climate encourages readers and writers to give feedback freely about the relevance of messages. Eventually, irrelevant messages will become extinct and the issue won't have to be raised very often. If readers never provide feedback to writers, the conditions will continue to create inboxes clogged with unnecessary information.

Chapter 6

Explicit business documents begin by preparing readers to read with purpose and understanding.

Readers must understand the information in a document beginning with the first word. The most effective business writing begins with explicit descriptions of the content and reasons the document is relevant for the reader at this time. That enables the reader to read with a clear purpose, increasing the reader's understanding and helping the reader organize the information meaningfully so it transfers into long-term memory.

This chapter explains the best practices that create clear, informative beginnings for documents so readers read with purpose and understanding.

Best Practice

Write e-mail subject lines using words that alert the reader to the contents, required action, or critical information in the e-mail.

Guidelines for this best practice:

1. Write subject lines using words that communicate immediately and personally to the reader.

2. Begin the subject line with words the reader could use later to retrieve the e-mail.

3. Convey the importance of the e-mail.

4. Write a subject line that meets the reader's needs.

5. Make sure your grammar, punctuation, and spelling in subject lines are correct.

Write subject lines using words that communicate immediately and personally to the reader.

Readers need a short statement about the e-mail that alerts them to the contents, required action, or critical information. Then they can decide what to do with the e-mail—open it now, prioritize it in their schedules, or forward it to someone else to handle.

Word the subject in a way that shows the benefit to the reader. You don't own your e-mail—your readers do. You just set up the e-mail message so they can act successfully, resulting in your success.

If you are responding to a request from the reader, use the reader's request in the subject line: "Ferndale data you requested." When appropriate, write "you" or "your" in the subject line; that shows you have included something of benefit to the reader.

Begin the subject line with words the reader could use later to retrieve the e-mail.

Begin the subject line with the words the reader might use later to retrieve it. Put the words that describe the subject first, then any additional information, as in these examples:

Instead of this: My suggestions for locating a vendor

Write this: Vendors – My suggestions for locating one

Replace the "Re:" and old subject line with a relevant subject line when you are using the "Reply" function. If you want to keep the thread of the conversation, use the same important words at the beginning of the subject line and add words relevant to your response after them.

Vendors – My suggestions for locating one

Vendors – My comments on your suggestions

Vendors – More about Deitrich

Convey the importance of the e-mail.

If the contents are very important or have a time constraint, consider stating that in the subject line: "Travel plans: IMPORTANT." "Meeting June 3 – ACTION: Need your availability today."

However, if you use such emphasis devices often, people will learn to disregard them when they come from you. In the same way, occasionally use the "High Priority" designation for e-mail, but avoid using it frequently. Readers will learn that you always designate your e-mail as "High Priority," so the flag won't be useful to you when you actually have a high priority message.

You might also capitalize an entire word for emphasis, but do so sparingly. Always capitalize words that normally should be capitalized in your subject line, such as "I" for yourself.

Make sure your grammar, punctuation, and spelling in subject lines are correct.

Incorrect usage (grammar, punctuation, and spelling) in subject lines is easily overlooked because writers forget to proofread them. Remember to check the subject line when you are proofreading the e-mail.

❖ Examples of good subject lines

Following are examples of good subject lines. The key terms the reader might use to retrieve the e-mail later are at the beginning.

> Brookside project Information
>
> Jane Smith interview confirmation
>
> Littleton contract – new ideas
>
> Meeting & agenda Jan. 10 – outline enclosed
>
> Meeting Jan. 10 – REQUIRED
>
> Recruiting in 2005 – I need your ideas

Best Practice

In the introduction, explain everything readers need to know to understand fully why they are receiving the document.

> **Guidelines for this best practice:**
> 1. Explain the context.
> 2. Explain the purpose for the document.
> 3. Write what's in the document for the reader.

An explicit introduction includes everything readers need to know to begin reading the document with purpose and understanding. Explain the context and reason the reader is receiving the document now. Do not include information in the introduction that is not necessary to understanding the content of the document, even if you feel it would enrich the reader. Do not include background information that isn't necessary for the reader to understand the content of the document and achieve your objectives.

Explain the context.

Why is the reader receiving this now? Readers should realize the relevance or importance of your document from its first words. The introduction should prepare readers to understand and remember the contents of the document so their reading is on track from the beginning.

Readers should not have to refer to another document or recall earlier conversations to be prepared to read the document. Don't assume readers will puzzle out the reason they've received your e-mail by reading the thread of e-mails that follows the message, and don't assume that because they requested something just yesterday, they will recall the request today.

❖ Example

The dates and references to meetings in the report introduction below will help the reader remember the request without searching through files.

> On July 15, Jane Reynolds requested suggestions of ways we can expand our Design Department while keeping our costs as low as possible. At a meeting on July 17, staff members discussed her request. This document lists five suggestions we believe will expand our Design Department and keep costs low:
>
> [document continues here]

Readers receiving this e-mail will know the context and content of the document immediately. They can begin evaluating the suggestions rather than trying to figure out why they received it.

Use the reader's words in the context.

When you prepared your notes for the document, you identified the reader's request key terms and wrote them on the first page. If your document is in response to a request, use those key terms at the beginning of the document. Summarizing the requirements in the reader's words shows the reader you are complying with the request and helps ensure that you are giving the reader everything he asked for.

❖ Example

This is the request for information in an e-mail:

Terry,

The production team needs some more concrete information about the users' workflow. Lester also mentioned that we don't know where the data comes from that they're using. We need to know the types of reports they'll generate after it's all said and done. Are there any forms they use to get their data so we can see the fields on them? Thanks.

Marie

This is the unclear type of e-mail we're all accustomed to receiving that Terry might have sent to Marie the next day:

Marie,

Attached...information about employee duties.

Terry

Marie may not recall her request or may forward the information to her production team without explaining the request or contents. The production team will have no idea what the e-mail is about and will begin a series of back-and-forth e-mails trying to find out what they are to do with it. Marie's forward without a message and Terry's curt statement both contribute to the confusion.

In addition, changing the key term from Marie's "users' workflow" to "employee duties" may throw her off when she reads the response. She may have thought she asked for something else, so a series of back-and-forth e-mail messages may ensue until she straightens out what she asked for and received. At the very least, this uninformative e-mail will require her to go back and read her request to see what she asked for, then skim the attachment to see what she received. That results in lost time and frustration for the reader.

Instead of that unclear e-mail, Terry should respond within an hour or two to Marie's request with the following e-mail:

Hello Marie,

I got your request and understand you need the following:

* more concrete information about the users' workflow
* where the data comes from that they're using
* the types of reports they need
* any forms they use to get their data

We'll work on it and get the information to you by tomorrow.

Terry

Terry's group works on Marie's request and the next day sends the information she requested attached to the e-mail message that follows. Terry's message states Marie's areas of interest using her words from the request and then explains the attachments that fulfill her request.

Hello Marie,

Yesterday you wrote that you need the following:

* more concrete information about the users' workflow
* where the data comes from that they're using
* the types of reports they need
* any forms they use to get their data

The information you need is in the attachment. It contains the following:

* a workflow diagram with all the users' activities
* a description of where the data comes from
* a list of the types of reports they need
* the two forms they receive from agents that contain data they input

After you've looked at it, call me or e-mail me if you have any questions.

Terry

Explicit business writing requires that all the parts necessary for an explicit message be there. We can't judge whether the reader will recall the request or realize what is in the attachment. To be explicit 100 percent of the time with 100 percent of the readers, the business writer should repeat the requester's words at the beginning of the response to the request and describe the attachments that fulfill the request.

Of course, when you are in a dialogue over an hour or two sending e-mail back and forth with a line or two of response, you don't need lengthy introductions. However, when time intervenes between responses or there is any chance the reader might not recall the context, always include it.

For e-mail messages, leave the previous e-mails that have information relevant to the current one in the thread of e-mails at the end. Delete any that are not relevant. However, don't omit the description of the context at the beginning assuming the thread of e-mails is all the reader needs.

Write the purpose for the document.

After you explain the context, describe the purpose of the document. How does it fit into the context? It likely provides the response or solution to the need described in the context. Write that.

❖ Example

This is an e-mail requesting a report:

> We're concerned that eventually the state EPA may say something about how the de-icing fluids are running off the tarmacs. Let's try to hold that off. Give me a report on what we are doing about the fluids, where they seem to be going, the likely state EPA response when we document where they're going, and some alternative means of disposing of the fluids if we're required to do so.

The introduction to the report should contain the context followed by the purpose. The context is in italics and the purpose statement is bolded for this example:

> Barton Airport currently allows de-icing fluids to run off the tarmacs onto the areas of grass bordering the tarmacs. We will be producing a document for the state EPA in another month describing the current status of disposal of the de-icing fluids. **The purpose of this report is to start the discussion of how we can try to handle EPA objections to our activities.**
> This report contains . . . [document continues here]

Often, a purpose statement won't be necessary. If you decide that the statement of the contents of the document will make the purpose clear, you may decide not to include a separate statement of the purpose.

❖ Example

This example repeats the report opening used in the previous examples. In this example, the opening has the context and statement of contents without a statement of the purpose. The context explanation is in italics; the statement of contents is bolded.

> Barton Airport currently allows de-icing fluids to run off the tarmacs onto the area of grass bordering the tarmacs. We will be producing a document for the state EPA in another month describing the status of disposal of the de-icing fluids. **This report contains our understanding of the likely EPA objections and three suggestions for handling them.**

Write what's in it for the reader.

If the document contains anything of benefit to the reader, include that in the introduction to increase the likelihood that the reader will read it and respond as you expect.

> I include a link to the company's Web site so you can see a demo of their software.

> You can use the timeline I've included to track the dates.

Best Practice

In the introduction, describe all actions the reader is expected to perform and any critical information the reader must know.

Guidelines for this best practice:

1. Write actions at the beginning and end.

2. Write critical information at the beginning and end.

Explicit documents state actions the reader is expected to perform and critical information the reader most know at the beginning of the document and at the end.

Write actions at the beginning and end.

Writing the action the reader is expected to perform at the beginning is important for four reasons:

1. Some readers never get to the end of the document. They may not realize an action is required.

2. For e-mail, many readers skim the beginning to see what the e-mail is all about and then go on to the next e-mail if they see nothing that requires immediate attention. If the writer describes the action only at the end, the reader may not discover it until later.

3. The beginning is a very strong position in a document. The reader will more likely remember the action and perform it if you place it at the beginning.

4. Putting the action in twice, at the beginning and at the end, increases the likelihood that the reader will complete it.

❖ Example

At the beginning, the writer states this:

> By Thursday at noon, send me your suggestions for the Friday meeting so I can use them as I plan the agenda.

At the end, the writer states this:

> I look forward to receiving your suggestions by Thursday at noon.

You may also write "ACTION" before the action statement at the beginning to ensure that the reader notices it.

Write critical information at the beginning

In the same way, write critical information the reader must know and remember at the beginning and end. You may decide to write "NOTE:" before the critical information.

❖ Example

At the beginning, the writer states this:

> **NOTE:** We will meet Monday morning at 10 a.m. in Conference Room C.

At the end, the writer states this:

> We'll see you Monday morning at 10 a.m. in Conference Room C.

Best Practice

Write a summary of the conclusions and recommendations at the beginning.

Guidelines for this best practice:

1. State the conclusions and recommendations at the beginning unless you have a strategic reason not to.

2. Introduce several conclusions or recommendations in a bulleted or numbered list.

State the conclusions and recommendations at the beginning unless you have a strategic reason not to.

If you have drawn conclusions or made recommendations that you believe the reader will accept, state them at the beginning. In unusual circumstances, you may believe the reader will need to read the evidence and logic that led you to the conclusions or recommendations before reading them. If so, state only the central idea in the introduction and write the conclusions and recommendations at the end.

If you state the conclusions and recommendations at the beginning, follow them with a statement of the contents of the rest of the document.

❖ Example of a single conclusion:

> We completed our investigation of the unusually large reduction in sales during February, concluding that the reduced sales resulted from the very cold month that kept people away from the store. The remainder of this report explains how we came to that conclusion.

Introduce several conclusions or recommendations in a bulleted or numbered list.

When you present several conclusions or recommendations at the beginning of the report, make them stand out clearly by presenting them in a bulleted or numbered list.

❖ Example

Below is a paragraph with the conclusions embedded:

> Our study of the literature has resulted in a series of recommendations: compile data on incidents of premature death, increased hospital admissions, and emergency room visits (primarily among the elderly and those individuals having cardiopulmonary disease); gather information about respiratory symptoms and disease, especially for children and individuals with cardiopulmonary diseases such as asthma; and study our admissions for decreased lung function in children and individuals with asthma to see if we should expand the respiratory services.

This is the same information broken out into lists:

Our study of the literature has resulted in three recommendations:

1. Compile data on the following:

    - Incidents of premature death

    - Increased hospital admissions

    - emergency room visits (primarily among the elderly and those individuals having cardiopulmonary disease)

2. Gather information about respiratory symptoms and disease, especially for children and individuals with cardiopulmonary diseases such as asthma.

3. Study our admissions for decreased lung function in children and individuals with asthma to see if we should expand the respiratory services.

Always introduce the lists of conclusions or recommendations with a sentence or phrase that identifies the contents of the list.

❖ Example of recommendations in an executive summary:

This example presents the recommendations in an executive summary with a brief summary of the rationales for each recommendation. The body of the report will then explain the rationales in detail.

The executive summary is not (1) an introduction, (2) a half page summarizing the report, or (3) highlights of the report. It is a brief version of the entire report, usually 10 percent of the length of the full report. Some suggest that, regardless of the length of the full report, the executive summary should be no more than two or three pages. Decide on the length based on your assessment of the reader and your objectives.

The example executive summary that follows lists the three recommendations and brief statements of the rationales. The report would then provide details about the rationales in the same order. Since the recommendations appear so close together, the writer has chosen not to list them in the executive summary before explaining them. However, the writer would list them at the beginning of the actual report.

Executive Summary

In October 2004, the Board requested that you investigate the costs and benefits of purchasing new equipment for the Sheridan plant. You completed the report and provided copies to us on November 20. Our evaluation of your report has resulted in three recommendations:

1. We recommend that you clarify the following three questions about the current and future use of the older equipment in the plant:

   - What is the projected period during which the equipment will remain usable?

   - When do you anticipate replacing the equipment?

   - What costs will be involved when the equipment requires repair because of age?

2. Explain whether the company's financial position likely will be the same, worse, or better at the time the equipment will have to be replaced.

   Your suggestion that we replace the equipment later requires that the finances be available at that later time to complete the replacement. Since the equipment will be worn and not usable by that time, if the money is not available to replace it, the company may be under a strain.

3. We recommend that you provide a detailed accounting statement explaining the costs of maintenance and repair over the period of time the company continues to use the old equipment. Compare that with the costs of replacing the equipment and maintenance and repair for the new equipment.

Best Practice

Write a clear statement of the contents at the end of the introduction so readers know what to expect and can prepare for reading.

Guidelines for this best practice:

1. End the introduction with a statement of the contents of the document.

2. If you are responding to the reader's request or questions, repeat the reader's key terms or questions as they appeared in the request.

3. Use exact numbers rather than "some," "several," or other imprecise term.

4. After you state the contents, begin a new paragraph for the first point.

End the introduction with a statement of the contents of the document.

After you finish describing the context for the document, state the contents. The statement of contents is your contract with the reader. It begins a pattern you'll follow throughout the document: State your point and then prove your point. Starting with a statement of the contents that will follow lets the reader see the overall framework before you fill in the details.

In the statement of contents, use the key terms exactly as you wrote them in your notes. The statement of the contents may be in any of the following formats:

1. If the document has one central idea, state it:

> In this report, I explain why we need to respond to this problem now.

2. If the document has two or more central ideas, state each:

> This e-mail contains answers to your two questions about Jim's trip next week and my suggestion for solving the problem of our inventory losses.

> In this report I explain two recommendations for the software purchase and a way we can convert the customer data to be accessible by any other system.

> Here are my thoughts on three issues: whether to hire a replacement for John, when we can reliably start selling health policies, and the strengths and weaknesses of the new workstations.

3. If the document has one central idea and the points explaining it are several paragraphs or more in length, state the central idea and list the points. Use the key terms you assigned to each of the points when you made your notes. Bullet out or number them if possible.

❖ Example

In an example presented earlier, the writer was responding to this request for a report:

> We're concerned that eventually the state EPA may say something about how the de-icing fluids are running off the tarmacs. Let's try to hold that off. Give me a report on what we are doing about the fluids, where they seem to be going, the likely state EPA response when we document where they're going, and some alternative means of disposing of the fluids if we're required to do so.

This is the introduction to the report. The earlier example showed the context and purpose for the document. This example adds a statement of the contents in a list:

Barton Airport currently allows de-icing fluids to run off the tarmacs onto the areas of grass bordering the tarmacs. We will be producing a document for the state EPA in another month describing the current status of disposal of the de-icing fluids. We have produced this report to start the discussion of how we can try to handle EPA objections to our activities. The report contains four explanations:

1. What we are doing about the fluids

2. Where they seem to be going

3. The likely state EPA response when we document where they are going

4. Three alternative means of disposing of the fluids if we're required to do so

---

The statement of contents uses the key terms from the reader's request, with the points presented in the same order, bulleted out to be clear. It changes the wording from the original "some alternatives" to "three alternatives," retaining the key term, "alternative means of disposing of the fluids."

If you are responding to the reader's request or questions, repeat the request key terms or questions as they appeared in the request.

When you prepared your notes in response to the reader's request, you identified the key terms for the request, issue, problem, or questions. List the key terms or questions from the request in your description of the contents of your response. That lets the reader know you are responding to the request and reminds the reader of the contents of the request.

❖ Example

This is the request:

> I understand we're having some problems with the Datamine program. Fran says the warehouse can't print customer pick slips at their location, FedEx orders still must be done manually, and no shipping summary reports are available as we had on our old software. What can you tell me about these problems? Thanks.

This is the introduction to the response:

> You asked what I can tell you about the three problems we're having with the Datamine program:
>
> 1. The warehouse can't print customer pick slips at their location.
>
> 2. FedEx orders still must be done manually.
>
> 3. No shipping summary reports are available as we had on our old software.
>
> My explanations follow.
>
> **1. The warehouse can't print customer pick slips at their location.**
>
> The warehouse can access and view order information but can't
>
> [e-mail continues here]

Use exact numbers rather than "some," "several," or other imprecise term.

Use exact numbers in all list openings.

Instead of this:
This document explains why we need to complete certain tasks before we begin the marketing campaign:

Write this:
This document explains why we need to complete these three tasks before we begin the marketing campaign:

Business writing should not contain vague words like "some," "several," or "a few" when the writer knows the exact number. Never use "a couple of"; write "two."

After you state the contents, begin a new paragraph for the first point.

After you state the contents, break for a new paragraph to begin the first point. As a general rule, don't put any words between the statement of contents and the first point. That confuses readers. If you want to add an explanation, put it in the introduction prior to the statement of contents.

❖ Example

This introduction has information after the statement of contents that should have been placed in the explanation before it. The misplaced information is in italics for this illustration:

This report describes the team's progress in locating a new plastics vendor. It contains three parts:

1. A list of the vendors we have identified

2. The strengths and weaknesses of each vendor

3. Our recommendation for the most satisfactory vendor and reasons for our choice

Ardmore Plastics was a reliable, inexpensive vendor, but the quality of their products has decreased in the last two years. We believe that is a result of their change in management.

1. List of the vendors we have identified.

We have identified four vendors that satisfy our criteria.

[document continues here]

The revised introduction follows. It contains the information about the vendor positioned before the statement of contents. The information is italicized for this illustration.

Ardmore Plastics was a reliable, inexpensive vendor, but the quality of their products has decreased in the last two years. We believe that is a result of their change in management. This report describes the team's progress in locating a new plastics vendor. It contains three parts:

1. A list of the vendors we have identified

2. The strengths and weaknesses of each vendor

3. Our recommendation for the most satisfactory vendor and reasons for the choice

1. List of the vendors we have identified.

We have identified four vendors that satisfy our criteria.

[document continues here]

Chapter 7

Explicit business writing has a clear framework that guides readers through the information.

Readers don't remember the words after they've finished reading a sentence or paragraph. They translate the words into an overall conceptualization of the information as they read and fit it into the base of knowledge they already have about the subject. That moves the information into long-term memory. Explicit business writing presents the information in a framework that helps readers translate the words into an overall conceptualization as they read. Without such a framework, the information remains in disjointed fragments and is easily forgotten.

This chapter explains best practices that create a framework for the document that helps readers understand and remember the information.

Best Practice

Write the information in clearly defined information blocks that the reader can read, understand, and remember, one block at a time.

Guidelines for this best practice:

1. Identify the blocks in your business writing.

2. Identify the Level 1 blocks in your information.

3. Identify the more detailed blocks in your information.

4. Keep each key term in its own block at first. Then combine blocks if necessary.

5. Let the key terms serve as headings.

Identify the blocks in your business writing.

Business writing must be 100 percent explicit for 100 percent of the readers 100 percent of the time. The changes we are seeing in the formats for business documents reflect this commitment. A page from an explicit business document today looks more like a bulletin than a novel.

The primary change is that business writers are presenting information in blocks the reader can identify easily. The blocks are marked explicitly using visual devices:

1. Headings signal new blocks of thought in e-mails, memos, letters, and reports.

2. Lists are broken out with numbers and bullets.

3. Rules (lines across the page) mark the beginnings of sections.

4. Information is placed in tables with lines that put information into boxes.

Each of these blocks focuses on a single idea and ends with a clear separation for the next block.

❖ Example

This is an e-mail without blocks. It is about a technical subject and uses jargon. You might think the problem is that it's technical. Actually, the fact that your mind can't identify the blocks makes it a jumble of words to you.

Hello Derrick,

A client is an institution or fund manager who uses CIS products and services our GIS relationships, but is not necessarily a customer of GIS. Each client listed under "Relationship" in the relationship-costing report contributes to the cost of the entire relationship. A relationship is an investment institution that is a GIS customer and may have many clients who service it: Relationship - DUT Bank #234000073, Client - Collerton Group. How did you get the annualized cost to be $465,000 for 2004? Our records show an annualized cost of $120,000 for 2004. Is DLTV Trust Company a GIS relationship or a CIS client that services that relationship? On the relationship costing report, August 2003 appears. Please clarify that the latest numbers you received were from 2004.

Lucy

The following e-mail contains the same information separated into blocks. You will identify the blocks immediately because they are marked by headings, indented lines, white space, and numbers. The writer adds openings for the blocks to let the reader know their contents. Even though it is technical and uses jargon, you have a better understanding of the content and could ask good questions to help you understand the subject.

Hello Derrick,

You asked about the meanings of "client" and "relationship" in our reports. My definitions follow. I also have three questions for you about DLTV Trust Company.

Definitions for "client" and "relationship"

Client

A "client" is an institution or fund manager who uses CIS products and services our GIS relationships, but is not necessarily a customer of GIS. Each client listed under

---

"Relationship" in the relationship-costing report contributes to the cost of the entire relationship.

Relationship

A "relationship" is an investment institution that is a GIS customer and may have many clients who service it. An example of this in your DUT bank relationship would be the following:

Relationship - DUT Bank #234000073
Client - Collerton Group

My three questions about DLTV Trust Company

1. How did you get the annualized cost to be $465,000 for 2004? Our records show an annualized cost of $120,000 for 2004.

2. Is DLTV Trust Company a GIS relationship or a CIS client that services that relationship?

3. On the relationship costing report, August 2003 appears. Please clarify that the latest numbers you received were from 2004.

Let me know if my definitions are clear and helpful to you. I look forward to receiving your answers to my three questions.

Lucy

You can see the blocks within blocks. Putting the information into blocks and introducing the blocks makes the text readable. This best practice explanation will help you define the blocks in your writing.

Identify the Level 1 blocks in your information.

When you prepared your notes for your document, you wrote key terms for ideas on Level 1, Level 2, Level 3, and so on. Each Level 1 idea makes up an individual block of its own. All of the Level 1 blocks together make up the entire document as one big block.

❖ Example

These are the Level 1 notes for a memo to employees about avoiding electric shock:

```
ELECTRIC SHOCK INJURIES

1 - CAUSES OF ELECTRIC SHOCK INJURIES

1 - PREVENTING ELECTRIC SHOCK INJURIES
```

Use the key terms as names for each block to help you write with focus later. The first block is the "causes of electric shock injuries" block. The second block is the "preventing electric shock injuries" block. The key term identifies the focus for the block.

Identify the more detailed blocks in your information.

Within the Level 1 blocks are smaller blocks: the Level 2 blocks. Within those blocks you may have smaller blocks: the Level 3 blocks.

❖ Example

These are all the notes for the memo to employees about electric shock injuries. Notice that the depth goes to Level 3.

```
ELECTRIC SHOCK INJURIES

1 - CAUSES OF ELECTRIC SHOCK INJURIES
  2 - frayed cords
  2 - broken plugs
  2 - broken outlet covers
  2 - open circuit breaker panels
  2 - light fixtures

1 - PREVENTING ELECTRIC SHOCK INJURIES
  2 - inspect equipment cords
   3 - frays
   3 - crimped wires
   3 - bare wires at the equipment
  2 - inspect equipment plugs
  2 - replace broken outlet covers
  2 - close circuit breaker panels
  2 - turn off lights to change light bulbs
```

When you look at the notes on the previous page, you can see the blocks immediately. Below are the notes with boxes around the blocks. The names to the right are the key terms for the blocks.

ELECTRIC SHOCK INJURIES   **Largest block name:**
                                           "Electric Shock Injuries"

1 – CAUSES OF ELECTRIC SHOCK INJURIES
 2 - frayed cords   **Block name:** "Causes of
 2 - broken plugs   Electric Shock Injuries"
 2 - broken outlet covers
 2 - open circuit breaker panels
 2 - light fixtures

1 – PREVENTING ELECTRIC SHOCK INJURIES   **Block name:**
 2 - inspect equipment cords   "Preventing
  3 - frays   **Block name:** "Inspect   Electric Shock
  3 - crimped wires   Equipment Cords"   Injuries"
  3 - bare wires at the equipment
 2 - inspect equipment plugs
 2 - replace broken outlet covers
 2 - close circuit breaker panels
 2 - turn off lights to change light bulbs

The electric shock memo will be most successful if every reader remembers these blocks:

- It was about causes of electric shock injuries.

- Electric shock injuries have five causes.

- There are five ways of preventing electric shock injuries.

- When inspecting equipment cords, we must look for three things.

Making these blocks clear as the reader progresses through the report will enable the reader to understand and remember the overall concept and the detailed concepts that make up the memo.

Keep each key term in its own block at first. Then combine blocks if needed.

As you write, keep each key term from your notes in its own block to help you maintain the focus for each block. Then combine blocks if the separated blocks are short and the relationship between them will be clearer if they are combined.

In an e-mail that has three distinct ideas, you might choose to have three short blocks in three paragraphs. After you write the three separate paragraphs, you may decide to combine them into one paragraph if doing so makes your points clearer.

However, don't be afraid of one-sentence paragraphs. Keep the blocks separate if each sentence contains a clearly separate idea.

As you write, let the key terms serve as headings.

You have the outline of your message in the key terms you wrote when you prepared your notes. The key terms give the blocks focus. As you fill in the information under the key terms, leave the key terms in place above the text you're writing to serve as headings. You may eliminate them when you create your final draft, but leave them in place as you write to help you maintain focus.

Best Practice

For each information block, write an explicit opening statement the reader can use to begin putting the block's details into a framework.

Guidelines for this best practice:

1. Write openings for the information blocks.

2. Use headings as opening devices.

3. Use the key terms in
    - the statement of contents at the end of the introduction
    - the headings
    - the openings for the blocks
    - the explanation text

Write openings for the information blocks.

Explicit business writing opens every block with a description of what is in the block. These openings signal to the reader, "I have finished the previous information block. This is the subject of the new information block." They let your reader see the big picture before you start to fill in the details, so when she finishes the document, she will remember both the framework and details.

Use the key term for the block in the opening. It will be the focus for the block until you explicitly show the reader you are starting a new block. The reader will keep working to fit your content into the focus of the block until you signal that you're changing focus. If you don't mark the change clearly, the reader will become confused.

❖ Example

These are the notes with blocks that were used as an illustration earlier. Each time a new level starts, the writer opens the new block of information with a sentence explaining the new block to the reader. In this way, the change and subject of the new block are clear.

ELECTRIC SHOCK INJURIES

Opening for the block that is the entire report here:

We can minimize electric shock injuries by knowing their causes and preventing them.

1 – CAUSES OF ELECTRIC SHOCK INJURIES

Opening for the first Level 1 block here:

Knowing these five causes of electric shock injuries will help us prevent them: frayed cords, broken plugs, broken outlet covers, open circuit breaker panels, and light fixtures.

2 - frayed cords
2 - broken plugs
2 - broken outlet covers
2 - open circuit breaker panels
2 - light fixtures

Use headings as opening devices.

Headings are ideal opening devices to show the focus of the block. The reader knows that a heading signals a new block, and the key term in the heading lets the reader know the subject of the new block. They create a visual outline of the message to help readers see the whole message as well as the parts. Headings are also valuable when the reader comes back to the document later to locate specific information. Use headings in all documents, including e-mails.

❖ Example

Using headings would have helped the writer of this report organize the blocks and would have helped the reader identify the blocks:

The most important action in successfully applying to an MBA program is to carefully follow the application procedures for selected schools. The application procedure requires that you first note the application deadline. Then, actually filing your application involves the completion of three activities: writing essays, obtaining letters of recommendation from your references, and obtaining academic transcripts. As stated, before you begin, you must note the specified deadline for applying. It is important that you send your materials well before that deadline. The first activity in actual filing of application is writing essays. Most schools will require you to write three or four personal essays. In one essay, provide your educational and personal background, your experience, and your goals. In another essay, discuss your perception of the importance of having an MBA degree from a particular school. Another essay should describe examples of your leadership, teamwork, and creativity. To ensure that your essays are complete and clear, ask family members, friends, colleagues, or professors to evaluate your essays. Obtain letters of recommendation from references. The references should be people who know you well. Discuss the objectives of the recommendations with them in advance to ensure a positive reflection of your abilities. Obtain academic transcripts. It is the simplest and least time consuming of the application activities. However, be sure you obtain the transcripts and send them in time.

The report that follows contains the same information, separated into blocks with headings that use the key terms.

This report explains the four actions you must take to apply successfully to an MBA program:

1. Note the time and requirements for submission.

2. Write essays to submit with the application.

3. Obtain letters of recommendation.

4. Obtain academic transcripts.

1. NOTE THE TIME AND REQUIREMENTS FOR SUBMISSION.

Note the time and requirements for submission so you submit the application before the due date with all the components the school expects you to submit. The time and requirements are normally found in the catalog or other materials you receive from the school, but if you don't have the information, call the school to obtain it.

2. WRITE ESSAYS TO SUBMIT WITH THE APPLICATION.

Most schools will require you to submit personal essays with the application. Write essays about the following three topics:

1. Your educational and personal background, experience, and goals

2. Your perception of the importance of having an MBA degree from the school to which you're applying

3. Your ability to lead, work in teams, and be creative

To ensure that your essays are complete and clear, ask family members, friends, colleagues, or professors to evaluate them.

3. OBTAIN LETTERS OF RECOMMENDATION.

Obtain letters of recommendation from people who know you well. Discuss the objectives of the recommendations with them in advance to ensure a positive reflection of your abilities.

4. OBTAIN ACADEMIC TRANSCRIPTS.

Obtain academic transcripts that you can send with the application, or have the school from which you graduated send the transcripts directly. This is the simplest and least time consuming of the four application actions. However, since it takes time for the school to process your request and send the transcripts, notify the school early so it sends them on time.

Use the key terms in the statement of contents, the headings, the openings for the blocks, and the explanation text.

The key terms are the threads that stitch the parts of the document together. They should appear in these places:

- The statement of contents in the introduction
- The headings
- The openings for the blocks
- The explanations

If the reader doesn't see the key terms at these points, or sees different key terms, the document will be more difficult to follow. Work to include the key terms in every one of the four places.

❖ Example

This is the first part of the document presented in the previous example. The key terms for the first Level 1 point are marked to show how the writer repeats the key terms to bind the report together:

This report contains explanations of the four actions you must take to apply successfully to an MBA program:

1. Note the time and requirements for submission.

2. Write essays to submit with the application.

3. Obtain letters of recommendation.

4. Obtain academic transcripts.

Repeated
key term

1. NOTE THE TIME AND REQUIREMENTS FOR SUBMISSION

Note the time and requirements for submission so that you submit the application before the due date with all the parts the school expects you to submit. The time and requirements are normally found in the catalog or other materials you receive from the school, but if you don't have the information, call the school to obtain it.

Best Practice

For lists with items that are each several paragraphs or pages long, open the lists with statements of the contents and then open list items with descriptions of the items' contents.

Guidelines for this best practice:

1. When the entire document is one list, clearly identify the list and list items.

2. Identify the key term for the list.

3. Open the document with the statement of contents using the number of items and key term.

4. Use an explicit opening format for each list item.

5. Identify other lists within the report that have longer items, and follow the same procedure.

Business documents commonly are composed of lists with items that are several paragraphs or pages long. This best practice explains how to open and write lists that have longer items. The next best practice in this book provides guidelines for opening and writing lists with shorter items.

When the entire document is one list, clearly identify the list and list items.

The largest list the business writer might have in a document is a list that is the entire document, as in these examples:

- A six-page report contains a list of three premium novelty giveaways with rationales for their use at the upcoming convention. Each premium is an item in the list.

- A three-page letter to the client contains a list of four features the writer suggests should be added to the product currently in development. Each feature is a list item.

Identify the key term for the list.

Select a name for the items in the list such as "conclusions," "steps," "characteristics," "recommendations," "problems," or "staff." Avoid using "thing," "topic," "aspect," or other words that don't precisely identify the items in the list. Settle on one name for the list items and use that consistently throughout your explanation.

Add the central idea of the document to the name for the items. If the list items are "benefits," the entire central idea key term might be "benefits of outsourcing." If the list items are "outcomes," the entire key term might be "outcomes of the move."

Open the document with the statement of contents using the number of items and key term.

When the entire document is a list, explain what is in the list in the statement of contents in the introduction. Specify the exact number of items and the key term that describes the contents, as in this example:

The audit revealed three problems with the procedure.

The exact number is "three." Do not use "a couple," "some," "a few," "many," or other imprecise term to introduce lists. The items are "problems." The key term is "problems with the procedure." Follow that statement with a list of the three items:

The audit revealed three problems with the procedure:

1. The time for incubation was too short to reveal effects.

2. Some portions of the sample started to deteriorate before other parts had finished growing.

3. The researcher had to check the samples every five minutes for eight hours, resulting in fatigue and carelessness toward the end of the process.

This report explains the three problems.

Use an explicit opening format for each list item.

Each list item is a block of information. Help your readers follow your explanation by opening each item using the same format; readers learn the format quickly and know when they are encountering a new item.

The most explicit format has three parts:

- The position of the item in the list (first, most important, and so on)
- Key term connecting the item to the subject of the list
- The item's point

These parts are explained in the paragraphs that follow.

State the position of the item in the list.

Items usually have some position in the list. The simplest positions are first, second, and third, or 1, 2, 3 and so on. However, each item may be in a position established by

- time ("the earliest," "the last")
- importance ("the most important," "the least critical")
- geographic location ("the farthest," "the highest")
- level of intensity ("the most intense," "the hottest")
- level of severity ("the most severe," "the worst")
- any other designations that have position

State the position for each item in the list.

❖ Examples

> The **first** characteristic . . .
>
> The **most important** qualification . . .
>
> The **earliest** reference to . . .

Prefer to use numbers to indicate the position rather than ordinals (first, second, and so on). Use ordinals when numbers are not appropriate.

❖ Examples

Instead of this:	The first step in the process is to identify the target market.
Prefer this:	1. Identify the target market.
Or this:	Step 1. Identify the target market.

Don't use ordinals alone (as in "First, we need to contact . . ."). The reader needs to know what the ordinal is the first of. Use the key term name you have given to the items in the list. In the following example, the name is "improvement."

❖ Examples

Instead of this:	First, the company needs a new logo.
Write this:	The first improvement our company needs is a new logo.

Use the list key term to connect the item to the list.

Connect the item to the list by writing the key term next.

❖ Examples

The most important **reason for installing security alarms** is . . . (The list key term is "reasons for installing security alarms.")

The fourth **floor of our building** houses . . . (The list key term is "floors of our building.")

The **difficulty with the vendor** that will create the fewest problems is . . . (The list key term is "difficulties with the vendor.")

State the point.

Finally, write the point of each item. Here are the complete openings for the list items with the points added and bolded.

❖ Examples

The most important reason for installing security alarms is **to deter future crime when professional burglars learn the building is secure.**

The fourth floor of our building houses **Information Services.**

The difficulty with the vendor that will create the fewest problems is **their habit of not cleaning up the work site.**

❖ Example

The result of using this explicit opening statement of contents for the list and explicit openings for the list items is a clear outline of the report, as in the example that follows. The list name is "qualities the principal we hire must have."

To be successful in curbing drug, alcohol, and tobacco use among our students, the principal we hire must have these three qualities:

1. The self-confidence to assert facts that teachers must know

2. Experience in motivating teachers to participate in programs

3. Knowledge of how to build a community of teachers committed to curbing drug, alcohol, and tobacco use among our students

The self-confidence to assert facts that teachers must know

The first quality the principal must have is the self-confidence to assert facts that teachers must know. The principal will hear teachers denying the problems. Our experience has been that a successful principal asserts the facts without being defensive or becoming angry. They are simply the facts.

Experience in motivating teachers to participate in programs

The second quality the principal must have is experience in motivating teachers to participate in programs. While every teacher would agree that the programs are important to the future of the school's drug, alcohol, and tobacco-use reduction program, most have too many duties already to participate actively. Their agreement with the need must be turned into a commitment to act. The principal must have experience in motivating teachers to participate in programs.

Knowledge of how to build a community of teachers committed to curbing drug, alcohol, and tobacco use among our students

The final quality the principal must have is the ability to build a community of teachers committed to curbing drug, alcohol, and tobacco use among our students. Teachers should understand that they are part of a community committed to the same goals. Their actions contribute to achieving the goals for the entire community. The principal must have the ability to build a community of individual teachers who believe that by acting as a team, they can curb drug, alcohol, and tobacco use.

Repeating the opening words may not sound right to you at first. Explicit business documents look and sound different from the writing business people are accustomed to. If you know how to write using the most explicit style, then you can choose to make it a little less explicit to suit your sense of what sounds good. However, the paramount goal is to have 100 percent comprehension 100 percent of the time by 100 percent of the readers, regardless of the writer's preferences.

Identify other lists within the report that have longer items and follow the same procedure.

Reports may also have lists within the report containing items that are several paragraphs or pages long. In that case, use the same procedure to introduce each list and open the list items.

1. Write a heading identifying what is in the list.

2. Follow the heading with a statement of the contents of the list using the number of items and key term for the list.

3. Use an explicit opening format for each list item. State the position, connection, and point of the item.

❖ Example

This example from the middle of a report is a description of the fourth problem in a list of six problems that make up the report. This example has only the opening for the list and first sentence of the first list item. The headings would be bolded as in this example.

Problem 4: **The nuclear safety risk assessments do not explicitly address survivability of equipment during accidents.**

The nuclear safety risk assessments do not address the following three issues that affect survivability of equipment during accidents:

1. Electrical equipment is affected by changes in temperature that occur during some nuclear accidents.

2. The hydraulic machinery will not operate if its liquids are heated past a certain temperature.

3. Temperature and humidity changes during a nuclear accident may cause meters to fail.

> Each of these issues is explained in the pages that follow.
>
> **Issue 1:   Electrical equipment is affected by changes in temperature that occur during nuclear accidents.**
>
> The first issue not addressed that affects survivability of equipment during accidents is the effect of temperature on the electrical equipment. [report continues here]

Notice that the headings are long enough to be explicit, and they use the same key terms in the same order as presented in the introduction. Write headings that are as long as they need to be to enable the reader to know clearly what will follow.

Best Practice

For lists with items that are a few lines long, break out the lists with numbers and bullets.

Guidelines for this best practice:

1. Identify all the lists containing items that are no more than a few lines long.

2. Use numbers for lists that have order. Use bullets for lists with short items that are in no special order.

3. Open the lists with clear statements of what is in them.

4. Keep list items within sentences together.

5. Keep bulleted or numbered list items together, and use the same format for every item in the list.

6. Indent the list and separate items that are two or more lines long by putting blank lines before and after the items.

7. Use simple filled circles rather than fancy bullets.

8. For nested or second-level bullets (lists within lists), use hollow circles or other simple bullets.

9. Consider bolding a key term or phrase at the beginning of each item to separate it and give it a distinct focus.

10. Keep list items in the same format.

11. Use a colon before a list if the colon ends a complete sentence.

Identify all the lists containing items that are no more than a few lines long.

Some of the lists in your documents will contain items that are no more than a few lines or a paragraph long. Always prefer to break out such lists with bullets or numbers. Leave list items in a sentence only if the items are shorter and breaking out the items will look odd because it gives them more prominence than is appropriate for them.

❖ Example of lists buried in a paragraph:

This example has lists buried within a paragraph, making it more difficult to follow:

> The Internal Conveyances Department is responsible for moving employees within the Rudolph Plant complex. Workers are taken from the gate to their work areas. Another function is that they are transported to storage areas to pick up supplies. They are taken to areas such as the cafeteria and training rooms. In addition, Internal Conveyances Department delivers internal packages, tools, and inter-office mail. The department is responsible for notifying Plant Maintenance as it notices lights burned out, spills, and other things that require maintenance attention. The system they use is able to store 400 maintenance tasks a day. Once this limitation is reached, the system must be shut down and paper maintenance logs kept, resulting in difficult management reporting.

The following revision is divided into two parts with these key term names for the parts: the "three responsibilities" part and the "software system" part. The first part lists three responsibilities. The writer has marked the beginning of the second part with a blank line and this opening: "The software system the department uses . . ."

> The Internal Conveyances Department has three responsibilities:
>
> 1. Moving employees within the Rudolph Plant complex to three destinations:
>   - their work areas
>   - storage areas to pick up supplies
>   - other areas such as the cafeteria and training rooms
>
> 2. Delivering internal packages, tools, and inter-office mail
>
> 3. Notifying Plant Maintenance as it notices lights burned out, spills, and other problems that require maintenance attention
>
> The software system the department uses is not adequate to handle its duties. The system is able to store 400 maintenance tasks a day. Once the system reaches this limitation, it must be shut down and employees must keep paper maintenance logs, resulting in difficulties with management reports.

Use numbers for lists that have order. Use bullets for lists with short items that are in no special order.

If the list is in a clear order, such as steps or items ordered by priority, use numbers. Writers also commonly number topics such as conclusions, recommendations, and guidelines that have longer items and complete sentences. If the listed items are short, incomplete sentences and require no special order, use bullets.

Open the lists with clear statements of what is in them.

Open the lists by stating the identifying names and the number of items. The following four guidelines are the same as the guidelines for items in longer lists described in the previous best practice:

1. Decide on a name to describe the items in the list: "issues," "problems," "steps," "recommendations," "questions," and so on.

2. State the exact number of items, such as "three recommendations." Do not use "some," "many," "several," "a couple," "a few," or other vague word.

3. State the subject of the list: "current and future use of farm ponds beside the airport" or "largest customers."

4. Normally put no text between the statement of what is in the list and the first item in the list.

For short lists of questions, of course, you might write something as simple as "Please answer the following questions." However, open every list, even short lists.

❖ Example

In the example that follows, the first list is "parts of the report." It contains two items: "questions" and "recommendations." Another list appears in the third "questions" item. The openings are bolded for this illustration.

Exact number   *Name for the items*

Your report contains descriptions of the disposal area for water discharged from the airport runways. We have **three questions about the current and future use of the farm ponds beside the airport:**

1. What is the projected time period that the ponds will   *Subject*
    be used to collect water?

2. Will the new owners allow use of the acreage for that
    purpose for an extended period?

3. Will this same acreage be sufficient to handle all the future
    water that might run off at this location? **In your answer,
    specify the following:**
                                        Simple opening

    a. What quantity of runoff can the acreage absorb
        in a 24-hour period?

    b. Into what channels will the acreage drain if it
        cannot hold the runoff?
Exact number   *Name for the items*

We also have **three recommendations for the water discharged
from the runways:**
                                        Subject

1. The water could be discharged to Lincoln Creek if the
    discharge meets water quality standards.

2. If only heavy metals are present, the contaminated water
    may be routed to the farm pond.

3. If an elevated level of nitrate is present, the water may be
    applied on the acreage reserved for that purpose so it seeps
    into the ground.

Keep list items within sentences together.

Business writers sometimes break up the lists in their sentences with words such as "in addition" or "as well as." This is an example:

> As well as Singapore, we have a growing customer base in Hong Kong, Kuala Lumpur, and Europe.

This is one list: "places where we have a growing customer base." The items are places: Singapore, Hong Kong, Kuala Lumpur, and Europe. The items in the list should be together to help the reader see and understand the entire list of places. The author could make a better list in either of two ways:

1. The first way to make a better list is to put all of the areas into one list: "We have a growing customer base in Singapore, Hong Kong, Kuala Lumpur, and Europe."

2. The second way to make a better list would be a better alternative if the preceding sentences had described Singapore as a place where the company has a growing customer base. The sentence following the explanation about Singapore would read, "We also have a growing customer base in Hong Kong, Kuala Lumpur, and Europe."

Keep bulleted or numbered list items together, and use the same format for every item in the list

Just as you should avoid breaking up lists within sentences, avoid breaking up the items that should be in a single bulleted or numbered list. Following is an example of a report that contains two lists presented in fragments that are buried in the text.

> Tom asked me to help Sue set up her own Bastion account and transfer the assets to Capitalmark. For this purpose, the Bastion IRA Application is enclosed. The first step is to transition the Custodial Bastion IRA, in both of your names, to a Bastion IRA, only in Sue's name. Also enclosed is the Letter of Authorization. This letter, signed by you, releases the custodial ownership of the funds into Sue's sole ownership. After you have filled out those forms, open the Bastion account with the other two forms: Capitalmark Bastion IRA Application to open a Bastion IRA at Capitalmark Investments for Sue and the Capitalmark Transfer Form to transfer Sue's account from Bastion to Capitalmark.
>
> To make it easier for both of you, I have completed the forms as much as possible. Please review them for accuracy. Sign and initial each form where indicated. Also, please complete the yellow highlighted areas (Sue's employment and so on).

This document is difficult to follow for two reasons:

1. The lists are embedded in the paragraph instead of being separated. The writer does not clearly define the two separate lists. The key term name for the first list is "steps you and Sue should complete." The key term name for the second list is "descriptions of the four enclosed forms."

2. The lists are not apparent because the list items are mixed together.

The first list is the "steps" list. The second list is the "descriptions of the four enclosed forms" list. To make this report clear, the writer should separate the information into two bulleted or numbered lists, open each list with a clear statement of the contents using the key term name, and clearly mark each item using a consistent format. Using the same format for every item in the list helps the reader see and understand the items as parts that make up the whole. It gives readers the big picture along with the details.

The two lists are separated in the revision that follows:

Tom asked me to help you and Sue set up her own Bastion account and transfer the assets to Capitalmark. I have enclosed four forms, filled out as much as possible. You and Sue should complete these three steps:

1. Review each form for accuracy.

2. Complete the yellow, highlighted areas (Sue's employment and other information).

3. Sign and initial each form where indicated. You must sign two forms and Sue must sign three.

These are descriptions of the four enclosed forms indicating which you and Sue must sign.

1. **The Bastion IRA Application.** The first step is to transition the Custodial Bastion IRA, now in both of your names, to a Bastion IRA in Sue's name only. This form will allow us to do that. You and Sue must both sign this form.

2. **The Letter of Authorization.** You alone sign this letter. It releases the custodial ownership of the funds into Sue's sole ownership. Sue does not need to sign it.

3. **The Capitalmark Bastion IRA Application.** This form will open a Capitalmark Investments account for Sue. She alone must sign the application form.

4. **The Capitalmark Transfer Form.** This form will transfer Sue's account from Bastion to Capitalmark. Since this is a form placing her funds from the standard Bastian IRA into the Capitalmark Investments account, she alone must also sign this form.

If you have any questions as you complete the forms, call me.

[contact information and closing here]

The lists are clearly separated and items are marked explicitly. These are the characteristics that define the lists:

1. The lists open with statements of their contents: "You and Sue should complete these three steps" and "These are descriptions of the four enclosed forms."

2. Each contains the number of items ("three" and "four").

3. Each specifies the type of items ("steps" and "forms").

4. Finally, every item begins in the same format. The "steps" list has verbs ("Review," "Complete," and "Sign and initial"). The "forms" list begins each item with the name of the form, bolded.

Indent the list and separate items that are two or more lines long by putting blank lines before and after the items.

Indent lists one-quarter to one-half inch from the margin of the previous text or list. If the items wrap (go on to the next line), help the reader to see the separate items more clearly by skipping a blank line between the list items. Consider setting the "Spacing Before" using Microsoft Word's paragraph functions, because it makes the text easier to edit. Set the spacing before at 12 points, about the height of one letter. If you have space constraints, set the spacing between the items at 6 points.

Use simple, filled circles rather than fancy bullets.

Use the more conservative bullets for all but the most informal documents. Fancy bullets are graphically appealing, but some readers may not like them because they are distracting and decrease the formal, business nature of the document. If readers find the bullets inappropriate or distracting, they may not be attentive to your message.

For nested or second-level bullets (lists within lists), use hollow circles or other simple bullets.

Hollow circles are suitable for second-level lists (lists within lists). Choose bullets that are visually weaker than the filled bullets you use for the first level to help the reader to see the outline organization.

You indented the first-level bullets one-quarter inch or one-half inch. Indent the second-level lists another one-quarter inch or one-half inch so the second-level list is indented twice the distance from the left margin.

Consider bolding a key term or phrase at the beginning of each item to separate it and give it a distinct focus.

One way to make the list items clear is to bold the key term at the beginning of each item to create an "inline heading." That gives the item focus and allows the reader to see the central idea of each item at a glance. These distinct key terms give the reader an overview of the entire list.

❖ Example

This is an example of a paragraph from a business proposal that contains lists the writer buries within the paragraph. Notice how dense the text appears and how difficult it is to read. Breaking the list out and putting bold key terms at the beginning would make it much clearer:

> Our Advertising Wizard software will provide the solution to your need to track advertising campaigns. It has a new reporting capability. You can better target your advertising dollars when you know what is working for your campaigns. Advertising Wizard provides the flexibility necessary to change your campaign depending on the report results. Reports can be run daily, weekly, or monthly and can be exported into a number of formats. The new interface will allow you to traffic your campaigns more quickly and efficiently. It has quick references. Even if your users have little or no trafficking experience, they can quickly understand where information is located and how to use Advertising Wizard to best suit your advertising needs. It has new content-sensitive help. Wherever your users are in the interface, they can click on "Help" and receive help targeted to their current position in Advertising Wizard. The new "Help" function will allow them to get started on Advertising Wizard without spending time in training classes. It has user-friendly features so your users can learn the basic features right in Advertising Wizard. When they are ready to use some of the more advanced tools such as Spotlight Reports, the Websoft Support Team is ready with online training classes, a robust knowledge base, and one-to-one personal support.

Following is the same paragraph broken out into lists. The list items have the key term of each item bolded to set it apart and make the content of each item clearer.

You may have the sense that this writing looks more like advertising than business writing. The reason is that over decades of writing to influence readers and gauging the results, advertisers have learned what communicates most clearly and quickly and have refined the art of writing to have an impact on readers. Now that business writing is focusing on writing to have impact, we are discovering the same techniques advertisers have been using for years.

Our Advertising Wizard software will provide the solution to your need to track advertising campaigns. Five new features make this the clear choice in available software solutions. ◄——— *List introduction*

Bold key terms

1. **The new reporting capability.** You can better target your advertising dollars when you know what is working for your campaigns. Advertising Wizard provides the flexibility to adjust your campaign using report results to make it more successful. You may run reports daily, weekly, or monthly and export them into 14 formats.

2. **User interface that allows you to traffic your campaigns more quickly and efficiently.** Advertising Wizard's user interface allows you to track your campaigns as they occur by selecting a single report.

3. **Quick references that show where information is located.** Even if your users have little or no trafficking experience, they can quickly understand where information is located and how they can use Advertising Wizard to best suit your advertising needs.

4. **Help with what users are doing wherever they are in Advertising Wizard.** One of the most important new features is the new content-sensitive help. Anywhere in the system, the user can click on "Help" and receive information targeted to that place in Advertising Wizard. The new help feature allows users to get started on Advertising Wizard without spending time in training classes.

5. **User-friendly features users will learn as they work.** When a user is ready to use some of the more advanced tools, such as Spotlight Reports, the Websoft Support Team is ready with

   - online training classes
   - a robust knowledge base
   - one-to-one personal support

Notice these parts of the rewritten proposal:

1. The writer uses simple filled bullets.

2. The items are separated with blank lines.

3. The writer states the concept of each item using the key term, bolded, at the beginning of the sentence.

Keep list items in the same format.

Keep all items in a list in the same format. If a list item begins with an action word, begin all the items with action words. If an item begins with an "ing" word, start all with "ing" words. If you indent numbered lists to one-quarter inch or one-half inch, you must indent to that position throughout the document, without deviation.

This writing sample contains two lists. The two lists are not in a consistent format and neither is broken out:

The documentation delivered and the associated process-improvement recommendations, along with associated process-performance-management program introduced, were the actions the consultant performed that resulted in improving Lawton Technologies' process standardization and improving sales force effectiveness, as well as better management of process performance.

The first list describes three things that were improved: process standardization, sales force effectiveness, and management of process performance. The second list is what caused the improvement: the documentation, process-improvement recommendations, and process-performance-management program. The examples that follow present these two lists using three formats. All three of the formats are acceptable in business writing.

For all of these formats, the text of list items should be no more than one or two blank characters from the bullet or number.

Format 1:   **Make the items complete sentences.** If one of the items is a complete sentence, capitalize the first words of all items and end with periods, even if one of the other items is not a complete sentence. However, if one item is a complete sentence, all should be complete sentences, if possible. An example follows.

> Three actions by the consultant were responsible for improving Lawton Technologies' process standardization, sales force effectiveness, and management of process performance:
>
> 1. She presented documentation with the software.
>
> 2. She presented process-improvement recommendations for the sales force.
>
> 3. She introduced a process-performance-management program based on the software.

The list in the first sentence contains very short items ("process standardization, sales force effectiveness, and management of process performance "), so the writer left it in a sentence. The items in the broken-out list are all full sentences with capitalized first words and periods at the ends. Some writers would like to eliminate the repeated "she" at the beginnings of the items. The formats below accomplish that.

Format 2:   **Use no end punctuation.** Do not use periods or other punctuation unless (1) one or more of the items is a complete sentence or (2) you are formatting the list as a sentence that is broken out (as in Format 3 below). Capitalize the first words of these items unless they flow as part of the sentence begun by the words preceding the list. In the example that follows, the sentence before the list ends at "efficiency," so the list items don't flow as part of the sentence and are capitalized.

> Three components of the consultant's efforts were responsible for improving Lawton Technologies' process standardization, sales force effectiveness, and management of process performance:
>
> 1. The documentation the consultant presented with the software
>
> 2. The process-improvement recommendations for the sales force
>
> 3. The process-performance-management program based on the software

The items do not have periods at the ends because they are not complete sentences.

In the example that follows, the list items flow as part of the sentence after "were," so the author chose not to capitalize them. A colon is not acceptable after "were" because the words before "were" are not a complete sentence.

The three actions by the consultant responsible for improving Lawton Technologies' process standardization, sales force effectiveness, and management of process performance were

1. providing documentation with the software

2. presenting process-improvement recommendations for the sales force

3. introducing a process-performance-management program based on the recommendations

---

Format 3:   **Use commas or semicolons and a period after the last item.** You may write the list as though it were a sentence divided up into items. If you do so, put a comma or semicolon at the end of each item and period after the last item. You may or may not write "and" at the end of the next-to-the-last item.

An example of this format follows:

The consultant improved Lawton Technologies' process standardization, sales force effectiveness, and management of process performance by

1. providing documentation with the software,

2. presenting process-improvement recommendations for the sales force, and

3. introducing a process-performance-management program based on the software.

Use a colon before a list if the colon ends a complete sentence.

Use a colon before a list only if the words preceding the colon are a complete sentence and you could use a period as easily as a colon. Business writers are commonly putting colons before lists even when the preceding sentence is not complete, but you should be aware that standard usage does not permit it.

INCORRECT:

Regardless of the benefits of the reductions, two impacts we know are that:

1. They will reduce morale.

2. They will make it difficult for us to function at peak level.

To use a colon, change the beginning to a complete sentence.

CORRECT:

Regardless of the benefits of the reductions, we know they will have two impacts:

1. They will reduce morale.

2. They will make it difficult for us to function at peak level.

Another way to correct the problem is to change the items and eliminate the colon. That would also eliminate the repeated "they will." Many readers prefer not to read repeated words at the beginnings of the items.

CORRECT:

Regardless of the benefits of the reductions, we know they will

1. reduce morale

2. make it difficult for us to function at peak level

Since the items are not complete sentences, the writer was correct not to put periods at the ends. Whether or not to capitalize the items' first words is left to the writer's discretion.

Best Practice

Present information in a clear visual blueprint so readers can see the organization as they read.

Guidelines for this best practice:

1. Use formatting to create an information blueprint.

2. Use headings that show a clear visual outline of the document.

3. Use white space to mark blocks.

4. Use rules (horizontal lines) to mark blocks.

Readers should be able to see a clear organizational pattern immediately when they look at an e-mail, memo, letter, or report. Explicit business writing uses visual elements to create an information blueprint that guides readers through the information, making it easier to follow and understand. Avoid having only dense paragraphs of text in business writing.

This best practice shows you how to mark blocks with visual devices.

Use formatting to create an information blueprint.

The old method of writing business reports placed the text into paragraphs, as in this example. It is the first part of a proposal for a bypass around the City of Tremont. The report has two major sections: "Direct Effects" and "Future Indirect Effects." Only the first section ("Direct Effects") is presented in the example that follows:

The city planners for the city of Tremont have reviewed your preliminary proposal for the bypass to be located west of Tremont. The bypass will allow through traffic on Business Route 14 (Main Street) to bypass the city of Tremont to avoid the congestion on Main Street that occurs now during peak traffic times. Our comments to help you prepare the final proposal follow.

The preliminary proposal indicates that traffic on Main Street would decrease by 35 percent when through traffic uses the bypass to avoid going through Tremont's business district. That could mean a reduction in sales for stores and restaurants along Main Street. The final proposal should address this concern by estimating the loss of patronage that might result. Discussions with owners of the businesses will help the builder learn how much Main Street business is generated from through traffic rather than from residents of the Tremont area.

Meet with Main Street business owners to learn how much the bypass will impact their businesses and include an analysis of the impacts in the final proposal. You also should suggest ways of informing traffic traveling through on Route 14 about Main Street stores and restaurants in the city in case they would patronize them to shop or eat. Explain the effects on use of the bypass if some people choose to enter the city to visit the stores and restaurants rather than use the bypass.

Another area of concern is that the Turtle River has flooded three times in the last ten years, resulting in some damage to houses and farm buildings in the town of Turtle River and surrounding area. Also, during times of drought, Millstone Creek has had a reduced flow that has created problems for farmers who rely on Millstone Creek for their cattle and hog operations. The final proposal should contain explanations of the impact of the shift in drainage on water flow in the Turtle River and Millstone Creek.

Contact the Corps of Engineers and use their resources to learn about the impacts of the shift in drainage on water flow in the Turtle River and Millstone Creek. Include statements in the final proposal that describe the maximum flow that would occur in the Turtle River when conditions are similar to those Tremont experienced when the Turtle River flooded in the past ten years. Also include descriptions of the minimum flow that would occur in Millstone Creek when drought conditions are similar to those Tremont experienced over the past ten years. Meet with the owners of the cattle and hog operations along Millstone Creek to learn the impact of reduced flow on their operations. Include a description of their assessments in the final proposal.

Future indirect effects will also have an impact.

[report continues here]

The writer has presented the explanations in paragraphs that all look the same, so the text contains no visual formatting to help the reader follow the points. Explicit business writing presents explanations in a visual blueprint so the readers can

1. see the parts immediately to begin internalizing the organization when they first look at the text

2. identify the beginnings and endings of ideas to help in understanding as they read

3. quickly locate parts later when they want to read them

The following report contains the same information, but the blocks are clearly identified with white space, lists, openings, and headings:

The city planners for the city of Tremont have reviewed your preliminary proposal for the bypass to be located west of Tremont. The bypass will allow through traffic on Business Route 14 (Main Street) to bypass the city of Tremont to avoid the congestion on Main Street that occurs now during peak traffic times. Our comments to help you prepare the final proposal follow, divided into comments about direct effects and future indirect effects resulting from the bypass.

DIRECT EFFECTS

The direct effects of the Tremont bypass projects will be from changes in traffic flow and in the land on which you build the bypass. The city of Tremont is concerned primarily about two effects:

1. The reduced traffic passing stores and restaurants along Main Street in Tremont that would impact their businesses

2. The likelihood that the bypass will shift drainage in the area west of Tremont from Millstone Creek into the Turtle River

Reduced traffic passing stores along Main Street

The first direct impact will be reduced traffic passing stores along Main Street. The preliminary proposal indicates that traffic on Main Street would decrease by 35 percent when through traffic uses the bypass to avoid going through Tremont's business district. That could mean a reduction in sales for stores and restaurants along Main Street. The final proposal should address this concern by estimating the loss of patronage that might result. Discussions with owners of the businesses will help you learn how much Main Street business is generated from through traffic rather than from Tremont residents.

Recommendations

1. Meet with Main Street business owners to learn how much the bypass will impact their businesses, and include an analysis of the impacts in the final proposal.

2. Suggest ways of informing traffic traveling on Route 14 about Main Street stores and restaurants in the city, in case they would patronize them to shop or eat. Explain the effects on use of the bypass if some people choose to enter the city to visit the stores and restaurants rather than use the bypass.

The shift in drainage from Millstone Creek to the Turtle River

The second direct impact will be the shift in drainage from Millstone Creek to the Turtle River. The Turtle River has flooded three times in the last ten years, resulting in some damage to houses and farm buildings in the town of Turtle River and surrounding area. Also, during times of drought, Millstone Creek has had a reduced flow that has created problems for farmers who rely on the creek for their cattle and hog operations. The final proposal should contain explanations of the impact of the shift in drainage on water flow in the Turtle River and Millstone Creek.

Recommendations

1. Contact the Corps of Engineers and use their resources to learn about the impacts of the shift in drainage on flow in the Turtle River and Millstone Creek.

2. Include statements in the final proposal that describe the maximum flow that would occur in the Turtle River when conditions are similar to those Tremont experienced when the Turtle River flooded in the past ten years.

3. Include statements in the final proposal that describe the minimum flow that would occur in Millstone Creek when drought conditions are similar to those Tremont experienced over the past ten years.

4. Meet with the owners of the cattle and hog operations along Millstone Creek to learn the impact of reduced flow on their operations. Include a description of their assessments in the final proposal.

FUTURE INDIRECT EFFECTS

[report continues here]

The formatting tools create a blueprint of the text for readers to help them follow the explanation and remember the points. The following pages explain how to use the formatting tools to create an information blueprint.

Use headings that show a clear visual outline of the document.

Choose to use headings wherever possible in all documents, including e-mails. Headings show the breaks for new blocks of information, alert readers to the point explained in the block, and give readers a visual organization pattern. Use the key terms from your notes as headings. Keep them in place as headings unless the text following is so short the reader doesn't need them to organize and understand the text. In that case, remove the heading in your final draft.

Example headings follow, arranged from strongest to weakest. Create your headings by adding or dropping emphasis devices (bolding, capitalization, larger font, and so on) to create the strength you want. Whatever format you choose, use the same format consistently through-out your document. All Level 1 headings should use the same format. All Level 2 headings should use a slightly weaker format, but one that is identical for all Level 2 blocks.

THIS IS THE STRONGEST HEADING, FOR LONG DOCUMENTS

Use this capitalized, bolded style as a Level 1 heading for long reports or the title for short reports. Don't use the same style for the title and Level 1 headings. If you use the style for the title, make the Level 1 headings weaker by not using all capitals. The example heading above is centered, all caps, bold, 14-point Arial or Helvetica font, 24 points (two blank lines) skipped before, and 12 points (one blank line) skipped after.

This Is a Good Heading for Level 1 in Short Documents

Use this style of heading for Level 1 in short documents or Level 2 in long documents when you've used the stronger heading above for Level 1. Make this heading flush left, bold, capitalizing only the first letters of words (except for prepositions, articles, or conjunctions), using the same font size as the body text, with 12 points (one blank line) skipped before and 12 points skipped after. You may choose to use Arial or Helvetica if the body text is in Times New Roman or a similar font. The differences in fonts are explained more fully in Chapter 10.

For Level 2 in Short Documents or Level 3 in Long Documents

This heading is weaker. It uses 12-point font without bolding, flush left, underlined, with 12 points skipped above and below it. You may choose to use Arial or Helvetica if you used the font for the other headings.

For even lower level headings, you may use italics or bold text positioned at the beginning of the line of text with only the first letter of the first word capitalized.

Follow these general guidelines for creating headings:

1. Do not use underlining with bolding or all capitalization. Use underlining with normal text only.

2. A strong heading uses several emphasis devices at the same time, such as a larger font, bolding, all capitals, and centering. The weakest headings use just one device, such as underlining or italics alone.

3. Skip blank lines before and after headings if the headings are on separate lines from the text.

4. Color is not generally acceptable for headings, so be sure your reader accepts the use of color if you decide to use it for headings. If you do use color, dark colors are the most conservative.

Use white space to mark blocks.

Use white space before and after blocks of text to show the level divisions (Level 1, Level 2, and so on). To show the divisions most clearly, indent the blocks so they have white space to the left. The example that follows uses white space to the left of two Level 1 blocks so the reader can see them easily and later skim the text to find information. The resulting text is more inviting to read and helps the reader understand the organization of the document. Colons are not necessary after the headings, but the writer could use them.

❖ Example

Introduction	As the projects that we have taken on move toward completion, we are receiving more requests for room usage.
	Marge, the facilities manager, coordinates room usage and keeps track of the rooms so everyone can use them freely without conflicts in scheduling.
Contents	This memorandum explains the following:
	1. Facilities Management's policy for room booking and usage that will help you as you plan your meetings
	2. Each manager's responsibilities when planning to book and use a room

Use rules (horizontal lines) to mark blocks.

Rules are horizontal lines that mark information block openings. Use rules for one level only, however. Using them with more than one level makes the document confusing. In the example that follows, the writer uses rules and white space to mark two Level 1 sections.

❖ Example

Introduction	As the projects that we have taken on move toward completion, we are receiving more requests for room usage.
	Marge, the facilities manager, coordinates room usage and keeps track of the rooms so everyone can use them freely without conflicts in scheduling.
Contents	This memorandum explains the following:
	1. Facilities Management's policy for room booking and usage that will help you as you plan your meetings
	2. Each manager's responsibilities when planning to book and use a room

Decide on visual formats and use them consistently.

Open the blocks in your documents using visual devices such as headings, indentations, and rules. Once you decide which visual devices to use for each level of block, use the same format throughout. Mark all Level 1 blocks in one way; mark the Level 2 blocks in another way. Readers need the consistency to follow your explanations.

❖ Example

This is the report presented earlier with several visual devices added:

COMMENTS ON THE TREMONT BYPASS PROPOSAL

The city planners for the city of Tremont have reviewed your preliminary proposal for the bypass to be located west of Tremont. The bypass will allow through traffic on Business Route 14 (Main Street) to bypass the city of Tremont to avoid the congestion on Main Street that occurs now during peak traffic times. Our comments to help you prepare the final proposal follow. They are divided into comments about direct effects and future indirect effects.

Direct Effects

The direct effects of the Tremont bypass projects are effects from changes in traffic flow and changes in the land on which the bypass is built. The city of Tremont is concerned primarily about two effects:

1. The reduced traffic passing stores and restaurants along Main Street in Tremont that would impact their businesses

2. The likelihood that the bypass will shift drainage in the area west of Tremont from Millstone Creek into the Turtle River

Effect 1:   Reduced traffic passing stores along Main Street

The first direct effect will be reduced traffic passing stores along Main Street. The preliminary proposal indicates that traffic on Main Street would decrease by 35 percent when through traffic uses the bypass to avoid going through Tremont's business district. That could mean a reduction in sales for stores and restaurants along Main Street.

The final proposal should address this concern by estimating the loss of patronage that might result. Discussions with owners of the businesses will help the builder learn how much Main Street business is generated from through traffic rather than residents of the Tremont area.

Recommendations

1. Meet with Main Street business owners to learn how much the bypass will impact their businesses, and include an analysis of the impacts in the final proposal.

2. Suggest ways of informing traffic traveling through on Route 14 about Main Street stores and restaurants in the city, in case they would patronize them to shop or eat. Explain the effects on use of the bypass if some people choose to enter the city to visit the stores and restaurants rather than use the bypass.

Effect 2: **The shift in drainage from Millstone Creek to the Turtle River**

The second direct impact will be the shift in drainage from Millstone Creek to the Turtle River. The Turtle River has flooded three times in the last ten years, resulting in some damage to houses and farm buildings in the town of Turtle River and surrounding area. Also, during times of drought, Millstone Creek has had a reduced flow that has created problems for farmers who rely on Millstone Creek for their cattle and hog operations.

The final proposal should contain explanations of the impact of the shift in drainage on water flow in the Turtle River and Millstone Creek.

Recommendations

1. Contact the Corps of Engineers and use their resources to learn about the impacts of the shift in drainage on flow in the Turtle River and Millstone Creek.

2. Include statements in the final proposal that describe the maximum flow that would occur in the Turtle River when conditions are similar to those Tremont experienced when the Turtle River flooded in the past ten years.

3. Include statements in the final proposal that describe the minimum flow that would occur in Millstone Creek when drought conditions are similar to those Tremont experienced over the past ten years.

4. Meet with the owners of the cattle and hog operations along Millstone Creek to learn the impact of reduced flow on their operations. Include a description of their assessments in the final proposal.

Future Indirect Effects

[report continues here]

Use headings and white space to write clear e-mail

Apply the same principles to e-mail. Use headings and white space to help readers identify the blocks in an e-mail. When you decide on a format, follow it throughout, precisely and consistently.

If you are using plain text for e-mails, use all caps for headings. Put a heading before each Level 1 explanation that is long enough for a heading. If you are sending a long e-mail, you may have Level 2 headings as well. Follow these guidelines:

1. Leave a blank line or two before all headings in an e-mail and one blank line after the heading.

2. Use the space bar to indent text that must be set apart. However, do not use the space bar for spacing in word-processed documents such as those written in Microsoft Word or WordPerfect. Instead, use the margin settings or tabs.

3. Use two blank lines to separate sections if that will make the separation of blocks of information clearer.

❖ Example

An example of a text e-mail follows. A text e-mail cannot show style variations in typography, so the writer marks blocks with words in all caps, numbers for list items, and blank lines between blocks.

Hi Barry,

Ferris and I have discussed the two changes to the system Jim proposed and have come to the following conclusions about allowing employees to make changes to their information and replacing HRTime with a centralized SQL database.

ALLOWING EMPLOYEES TO MAKE CHANGES TO THEIR INFORMATION

We agreed that we will not develop the features that allow employees to make changes to their information in the HRTime system for two reasons:

1. We would have to work out the data issues you brought up at the last meeting before we could design the function.

2. We would have to make changes to the DataTrack system to keep the two in sync. That would double the amount of work involved.

REPLACING HRTime WITH A CENTRALIZED SQL DATABASE

We are thinking that it would be a good idea for us to investigate replacing HRTime with a centralized SQL database for three reasons:

1. Management Services and Employee Self Services are already using an SQL database, so some of our data is already in that format.

2. HRTime is seven years old now, so we expect that it will require updating in these two areas if we don't replace it:
    * number of records it will permit
    * size of the client-code field

3. An SQL database will allow us to keep all of the data from DataTrack and the other systems in sync.

I'll keep you informed about our continuing discussions concerning both of these issues. If you have any questions, call me or e-mail me.

Melinda
Melinda.Barron@triptechs.com
X4328

Best Practice

Use tables to organize information so readers
can place the details into a clear framework.

Tables present a visual diagram of the information by showing
blocks clearly. Always choose to put information that has a matrix form
into a table. A matrix consists of a row of headings across the top with
characteristics of the subject and a column of other characteristics on the
left side. If you draw imaginary lines from the topics at the top
downward and from the topics in the left column rightward, the place
where the lines intersect would contain the information with the
characteristics of both the topic from the top row and the topic from the
left column.

❖ Example

This is an example of data that would be more clearly presented as a
table because it is in a matrix:

> Your daily activities must be restricted to the following limits. You
> may have no more than six hours of allowed driving, meaning driving
> that has been assigned to you, to include traveling to the drop-off
> destination and returning, as well as other activities involving the
> vehicle, such as vehicle maintenance. That time is compensated at
> $17 per hour. You may have a total of two hours of non-driving duties
> per day. Those duties will be mostly paperwork, but may include
> meetings, training, and other such non-driving activities. They do not
> include lunch, although the time will include breaks. This time will be
> compensated at $17 per hour. Finally, you may have four hours of
> overtime maximum per day. It must be assigned by your supervisor
> and approved before you begin the overtime activity. The fact that it is
> overtime activity must be noted on your time report even though the
> total comes to over eight hours per day showing there must have been
> some overtime. Overtime is compensated at $25.50 per hour.

The following example presents the same information in a table
format. It is much easier to read, and the reader can locate information
of interest to him instantly. The writer has broken out and bolded the
key terms to make the organization and the thought blocks clear.

ACTIVITY	DAILY TIME LIMIT	COMPENSATION
Allowed driving Allowed driving is driving that has been assigned to you, to include traveling to the drop-off destination and returning, as well as other activities involving the vehicle, such as vehicle maintenance.	6 hours	$17 per hour
Non-driving duties Non-driving duties are mostly paperwork, but may include meetings, training, and other such non-driving activities. They do not include lunch, although the time will include breaks.	2 hours	$17 per hour
Overtime Overtime must be assigned by your supervisor and approved before you begin the overtime activity. The fact that it is overtime activity must be noted on your time report even though the total comes to over eight hours per day showing there must have been some overtime.	4 hours	$25.50 per hour

You may combine tables with text, headings, and rules to present the key terms and information breaks clearly. Just make sure the key terms stand out and the information in the cells presents the data clearly.

❖ Example

Following is the same text presented in the previous example, but using a different format. Notice that the key terms still stand out through the use of white space and bolding. The information is separated into clear blocks by white space and lines.

ACTIVITY: Allowed driving

Allowed driving is driving that has been assigned to you, including traveling to the drop-off destination and returning, as well as other activities involving the vehicle, such as vehicle maintenance.

DAILY TIME LIMIT	6 hours
COMPENSATION	$17 per hour

ACTIVITY: Non-driving duties

Non-driving duties are mostly paperwork, but may include meetings, training, and other such non-driving activities. They do not include lunch, although the time will include breaks.

DAILY TIME LIMIT	2 hours
COMPENSATION	$17 per hour

ACTIVITY: Overtime

Overtime must be assigned by your supervisor and approved before you begin the overtime activity. The fact that it is overtime activity must be noted on your time report even though the total comes to over eight hours per day showing there must have been some overtime.

DAILY TIME LIMIT	4 hours
COMPENSATION	$22.50 per hour

Best Practice

End documents with a conclusion that helps readers achieve your objectives.

Guidelines for this best practice:

1. Restate the points if that will help the reader understand and remember.

2. End cordially.

3. Explain the next step.

4. Write conclusions that achieve objectives.

Explicit writing includes a conclusion that pointedly helps achieve your objectives with the specific reader. Follow these guidelines:

1. **Restate the points if that will help the reader understand and remember.**

   - Restate the Level 1 points in the conclusion if that will help the reader see the points together, especially if your message builds an appeal or argument leading to a conclusion or action. If you are not building to a conclusion and the message is short, you likely should not restate the Level 1 points because the restated points will appear forced and inappropriate.

   - Introduce no new concepts in the conclusion.

   - Write anything that will help the reader understand the situation you explained at the beginning, now that he has finished reading the document.

2. **End cordially.**

   - End with the same reassurances you used at the beginning if you included a buffer in the introduction to reduce a negative reaction. That shows your sincerity.

- End with your interest in being helpful. Write, "Call me or send me an e-mail if you have any questions" or "I will help in any way I can." Saying you are available and willing to help communicates your wish to cooperate and builds a partnership spirit with your reader.

- Repeat your appreciation of the reader's efforts or help, even if you stated that in the introduction. Don't fabricate something if you have nothing real and concrete to say in appreciation.

3. **Explain the next step.**

- Explain what you will do next if you are the one to take the next step.

- If the reader is to take the next step, describe the step and explain your willingness to help, your appreciation for the reader's effort, or your anticipation of the reader's actions.

- Include follow-up information about the next steps: who, what, when, where, and how.

- Include a feedback loop (explained in the next best practice) to make sure the reader completes the next step.

4. **Include contact information in correspondence.**

- Provide your phone number, extension, and e-mail address.

Write conclusions that achieve objectives.

Below is a list of the common business objectives paired with possible types of conclusions:

- **Objective: The reader received what she requested.** Ask the reader for comments on whether the content satisfied her request. Offer additional information or help if you have it.

- **Objective: The reader will follow a procedure.** End with the final state describing what will result from following the procedure. Then include your contact information and openness to help if the reader can't follow the procedure or if the procedure doesn't work.

- **Objective: The reader will know something.** Repeat the key information the reader must remember. If you include many facts or concepts, summarize them as they pertain to the issue you reviewed in the context at the beginning.

- **Objective: The reader will act.** Restate the action the reader is expected to perform as introduced in the beginning of the document. Include what the reader must do, by what time and date, and to what specifications. If the action is important or you are not sure the reader will follow through, include some way of getting feedback after the reader acts.

- **Objective: The reader will decide.** Summarize the contents as they pertain to the decision the reader must make. Provide insights that might help the reader now that he has read the message. Include a feedback loop for the reader to let you know that the reader did decide.

- **Objective: The reader will believe, be persuaded, or feel committed.** End with a stimulating appeal that explains explicitly what you want the reader to believe. Make the appeal meaningful and personal for the reader.

Best Practice

Include feedback loops that reflect the importance of the content and your assessment of the likelihood this reader will understand or act as expected.

Guidelines for this best practice:

1. Use feedback loops that are less concrete when you know this reader will follow through, and the actions are not critical to the company.

2. Use concrete feedback loops when you don't know that this reader will follow through, or the actions are critical to the company.

3. Always follow up on your requests for a response.

4. Use a more direct medium when a reader consistently won't respond; then escalate the problem to administration.

Develop the habit of including a feedback loop in your e-mails, memos, and letters. The feedback loop is the means by which you will know that the person you contacted has received your correspondence, read it, and achieved your objectives. The more important the message or the greater the risk involved in miscommunication or failed action, the more concrete the feedback loop should be.

Use feedback loops that are less concrete when you know this reader will follow through, and the actions are not critical to the company.

A less concrete feedback loop allows the reader to make decisions about whether to respond, in what medium to respond, when to respond, and what to include in the response.

❖ Examples

Let me know what you think.

If you need clarification, call me.

Give me any alternatives you can think of.

You might not ask for the feedback response or may use only general instructions for the feedback when

- you know the reader well and are confident the reader will respond appropriately

- the message is easy to understand

- the message is not vital, and there is no risk to you or the company if the reader doesn't understand or act as expected

These are the characteristics of a more open feedback loop:

- The reader may decide how and when to respond.

- It leaves open alternatives for method and content of the feedback response.

An example of a less concrete feedback loop follows:

Juan,

The conference call with the management consultant is scheduled for Friday, September 24, at 2:00 p.m. We'll each give her any questions we have about this method of reorganizing the department. Let me know if you have any questions about it.

    Frank

Use concrete feedback loops when you don't know that this reader will follow through, or the actions are critical to the company.

A concrete feedback loop directs the reader to respond in specific, concrete ways. Require concrete feedback when there is a possibility of miscommunication, you are concerned the reader may not respond as you wish, the message is very important, or there is risk involved if the reader fails to understand or act.

The concrete feedback loop

- requires a single method of response

- requires response by a certain date or time

- allows no alternatives for the response

- specifies in detail what the reader must provide in the response

- has observable, measurable means to ensure the reader complied

❖ Examples

Send me an e-mail with your responses to each of the three questions by Friday at 2:00 p.m.

Call me this afternoon to discuss the contents of this memo.

Send it by 4:30 p.m. today and e-mail me letting me know when the shipment went out. Include the tracking number.

The following e-mail uses an example of a concrete feedback loop. Notice that it is similar to the previous email, except that Frank has decided that the reader must have good questions for the consultant and must not miss the call. As a result, he inserts two feedback loops: one to be sure the reader has formulated questions and the other to be sure the reader will be available for the conference call.

Juan,

The conference call with the management consultant is scheduled for Friday, September 24, at 2:00 p.m. We'll each give her any questions we have about this method of reorganizing the department. E-mail the questions you will ask the consultant by Wednesday afternoon so I can send you my comments about them. Call me Friday at 1:30 so we can talk about our plans for the call.

Frank

Always follow up on your requests for a response.

You are teaching the reader about yourself every time you send or respond to an e-mail message or letter. Requesters may learn you respond promptly and accurately, or they may learn they cannot rely upon you to respond promptly or as they expected. Readers may learn that your messages are always clear, to the point, and relevant, or they may learn that your messages are usually unclear, rambling, and filled with irrelevant information. The expectations you set up over repeated e-mails and letters shape the views business people have of you and their correspondence from you.

If you ask for a response, follow up to make sure you receive the response. Make a note about it to remind yourself to check on it. If you don't receive a response, follow up by contacting the person by phone or in a visit. Your readers will learn that if they don't respond to your e-mail in the time you expected, you will be contacting them using a more direct medium. They will be more likely to respond promptly in the future. If they learn you won't follow up, they will be more likely to ignore your requests because they know there will be no consequence.

Never request something and then fail to follow up on the response to your request.

When a reader consistently won't respond, use a direct medium; then escalate the problem to administration.

When you need a response from the reader, send only one reminder e-mail. Then contact the reader through some other medium, such as a phone call or visit. If you just keep sending reminders, readers will learn they don't have to respond right away; you'll send another reminder in a day or two.

If the reader doesn't respond after the reminder and personal contact, it is an administrative problem. Your company or agency must not tolerate the practice of not responding to e-mail. It is not your responsibility to cajole the reader into responding. Administrators at the level above you must talk with the person not responding or to that person's immediate superior. If the company or agency is clear about the need to respond to requests, the offending behavior will rapidly become extinct.

Chapter 8

Explicit business writing has explanations that are so clear they cannot be misunderstood.

The goal of explicit business writing is to have 100 percent comprehension by 100 percent of the readers 100 percent of the time. To achieve that consistent level of clarity, business people must write in ways that are notably different from the ways they may have been taught to write in school and college.

Business documents that communicate successfully are more concrete and detailed. Sentences are shorter, using simple, everyday language any reader can understand. Key terms are used consistently, even if they are repeated several times in a single paragraph.

The result of this care in writing explicitly is that readers understand, remember, and respond as expected. The explicit writing creates a communication infrastructure that helps writers, readers, and the business or agency succeed.

This chapter explains the best practices that result in explicit business writing that is so clear it cannot be misunderstood.

Best Practice

Write concrete, precise, detailed descriptions of problems and issues.

Guidelines for this best practice:

    1. Write concrete descriptions of problems.

    2. Write concrete descriptions of issues.

Poorly written descriptions of problems the writer is experiencing and issues the writer wants the reader to understand result in miscommunication and a series of e-mails as the reader tries to understand the problem or issue.

Write concrete descriptions of problems.

Write concrete descriptions of problems, not generalizations. Generalizations are statements that are abstract; they state conclusions without including the support. Imagine receiving an e-mail with one of these generalizations and no concrete details:

> **The system doesn't work.** *(Details are missing: What difficulty did you have? At what point in the system were you? What was on your screen? What did you do? What error messages did you see? What did you try that didn't work?)*

> **We can't finish.** (What can't you finish? Why? What do you need now? What do you want me to do?)

This is a poorly written description of a problem:

Sid, the new password didn't work. Send me instructions.

Larry

Sid will have no idea what the problem is or what Larry wants him to do about it. In this case, if Sid sends a new password, Larry will be frustrated because the problem isn't with the password, but Sid couldn't tell that from this e-mail. Larry hasn't been clear about the problem or his need.

The following is a more explicit description of the problem and request. This is an example of the detailed description of an issue or problem business writers should prepare. You'll see all the detail Larry left out of the version above, and you'll understand why Sid's sending a new password would have resulted in frustration for both Larry and Sid and a series of e-mails to identify the real problem.

Sid,

I used the new password you gave to me. It did get me to the opening menu. However, when I clicked on Option 2 to access the client records, I saw this message: "You do not have permission to access this option." I clicked on "OK" under that message and I went to the main menu again.

Please let me know if I need a new password, permission to use the option, or some special instructions I'm now missing.

Thanks for your help.

Larry

As it turns out, the password worked, but MIS needed to change the permissions to allow Larry to access the customer records. Sid can now have MIS correct the problem and advise Larry in one e-mail that the problem has been solved.

When you must write the description of a problem, avoid writing generalizations without details. Write every detail about the problem the reader may need to know to understand what happened. Start from the point at which the problem began and explain the concrete occurrences using sense details (what you saw, heard, felt, tasted, or touched). If you write generalizations, follow them with details.

Assume the reader will not get the idea. Ask yourself, "What might the reader miss in my description?" Explain that more fully.

Write concrete descriptions of issues.

When you are writing the description of an issue, provide the history the reader needs to understand the situation. Explain concretely what people said or did, stating words spoken and descriptions of actions. Avoid writing just generalizations or conclusions because the generalizations won't help the reader understand the specifics, and your conclusions may not be correct. Include all the evidence the reader needs to know to understand the problem by knowing the details.

This poorly written description of an issue contains only generalizations:

Hi Brenda,

Well, it looks like they're going to need more time. I can't figure this one out. Oh well.

    Sue

Brenda may recall what Sue is talking about, but she may not. Who are "they"? What do they need more time for? How much time is "more time"? What was Sue's response to them? What is Brenda to do about it?

Here is a more detailed description of the issue. You'll see all the detail Sue left out that was important for Brenda to know.

Hi Brenda,

I told you I'd talk to Leyton Associates about the audit to find out whether they'll have the report this Friday as we expected, so I called this morning. Barry Fitzsimmons told me that they have finished the audit, but will need another week to write the report. I told him I would explain that to you and let you contact him about whether that is satisfactory. His e-mail address is barry.fitzsimmons@leyton.com.

I don't believe they need the rest of this week and all of next week to complete a short report. I didn't ask him for a rationale.

Sue

Sue included all of the facts that led up to this document, even if she thought Brenda might know some of them. You may begin such descriptions with, "As you know . . .," but assume the reader may not know or may have forgotten. Put the issue into context.

Never omit the background and detail because you're concerned you might offend the reader by telling her something she already knows. If the reader really is offended, it's because the corporate culture hasn't yet evolved to the point at which everyone expects and encourages explicit writing above all else. The only way to build that culture is to write explicitly 100 percent of the time and encourage others to write explicitly, even if people have to mature into accepting that.

Best Practice

Write requests that state directly, unambiguously, and completely what you are requesting.

Guidelines for this best practice:

1. Write direct, unambiguous request statements.

2. Write detailed, explicit explanations of the requests.

If you often find yourself frustrated because readers don't provide you with the information you need or don't complete the activity as you expected, the chances are very good that you share some of the burden for the failures. The more explicit your requests, the more likely you and the reader will be satisfied when the requests provide what you want. The more general and vague the requests, the more likely you'll be frustrated by having to repeat requests and wait for second responses.

Write direct, unambiguous request statements.

Business writers are sometimes worried about being too direct. They feel they're being too blunt, bossy, or intimidating. As a result, they make vague statements hoping the reader will get the idea without being offended: "I could use your budget figures when you have a moment to send them." What she really means is, "I need your budget figures by tomorrow afternoon to submit the report on time." Someone writes, "We'd appreciate your comments at the meeting," when he really means "You have to attend this meeting to explain why you've suggested we change vendors."

Whether a reader feels you're bossy won't be determined by writing direct or indirect sentences. You establish a relationship over time in the way you either partner with the reader and develop a feeling of good will, or maintain a distant tone with the reader and convey a sense of disinterest in the reader's needs or efforts. If the reader believes you regard him highly, appreciate his work, and are looking out for his best interests, he will tend to accept anything you say with at least openness and cooperation. If the reader feels you have no regard for him, he likely will view anything you write with suspicion, including the vague, non-direct statements. They may actually sound devious to this reader.

Build the good will and partnering spirit over time through the other statements you make in your correspondence: "I appreciate your willingness to help," "Thanks for taking the time to send the information to me," "Your comments about the marketing campaign were great. Thanks." Then you can be direct about what you need, stating explicitly what you want:

> I need the budget figures by tomorrow afternoon to prepare for Friday's meeting.
>
> You must come to this meeting to explain your suggestion.
>
> Please give me your rewritten draft when we meet on Wednesday.

Include your rationale for the request to help the reader understand why you are making it. Include positive statements about the reader:

> Your suggestion is really important and everyone should hear about it. You must come to this meeting to explain it.
>
> Please give me your rewritten draft when we meet on Wednesday morning. Thanks for the work you've been putting in on this report. The end is in sight.

Write detailed, explicit specifications for requests.

Write descriptions of requests in detail. Include the following:

- all parts of the action you want the reader to complete
- the time by which it must be completed
- the conditions under which it must be completed

Anticipate errors that might be present in what the reader gives you and write additional explanations that will reduce the chances of the errors occurring.

❖ Example

A poorly written request for action follows:

> Team,
>
> I'll need the paperwork for the conference ASAP!
>
> T.B.

This is a better request. It contains a rationale and the action, time, and conditions, in detail.

> Team,
>
> I need the following paperwork for the conference by Wednesday afternoon so I can submit it to purchasing:
>
> 1. Your travel request filled out and signed
>
> 2. Your registration for the conference filled out and signed
>
> 3. A list of anticipated purchases you might make, including descriptions of the items and estimated amounts
>
> Send them through company mail, not USPS, so we can be sure they're here on time. My mail drop is Corporate 5483.
>
> T.B.

Best Practice

Use key terms consistently.

> **Guidelines for this best practice:**
>   1. Use the same key terms consistently throughout.
>   2. Repeat key terms in the text to show how the concepts fit together.

Use the same key terms consistently throughout.

Once you introduce a concept using a key term, don't change the key term; the reader may assume that the new key term stands for a new concept. That creates confusion.

❖ Example

This is the opening sentence for a block of information:

> Holding training sessions in several remote sites would be better than bringing people in from the field to the home office.

These are the key terms:

> "training sessions," "several remote sites," "bringing people in from the field," and "home office."

You may have learned in high school English that you should avoid repeating words. That is true for words that carry no critical meaning, such as "in," "from," "better," and all the other glue words that hold together the key terms. However, don't use alternative words for the key terms. Use them repeatedly without changing them.

In the example sentence above, "remote sites" is the key term. See the confusion that results when the writer changes the term in the next sentences of the paragraph. The key terms are bolded for this illustration.

> Holding training sessions in several **remote sites** would be better than bringing people in from the field to the home office. A **distance learning location** would have facilities that could enhance the experience. One way to ensure that our presentations are consistent is to have **regional training classrooms** with the same instructors going from region to region to meet with employees.

The reader is left wondering whether "remote sites," "distance learning location," and "regional training classrooms" are two or three different options. Each seems to be opening a new concept. Once the writer settled on "remote sites," she should have locked in that key term. The writer also changes another unnecessarily. "Training" should appear consistently throughout. Instead, the writer changes to "distance learning," "experience," "presentations," and "meet with employees."

The writer uses the key terms consistently in the following revision:

> Holding **training** sessions in several **remote sites** would be better than bringing people in from the field to the home office. **These sites** would have facilities that could enhance the **training**. One way to ensure that our **training** is consistent is to have a **remote site** in each region with the same instructors going from region to region to do the **training**.

Repeat key terms in the text to show how the concepts fit together.

Each time you repeat a key term and add new information, the reader will be able to fit the new information into the overall picture. That clarifies the writing because the reader is able to assemble the puzzle pieces into a complete picture, one concept at a time.

❖ Example

This paragraph is difficult to follow because it does not repeat the key terms to help the reader follow the message. The key terms are "downsizing" and "communication between management and employees." You will see them in the opening, but not in the paragraph.

When a company considers **downsizing, good communication between management and employees** is very important. Employees must understand reasons for company changes, and understanding reduces feelings of insecurity and rejection. Often, management is unclear and tries to hide the actual dimension of business transitions by withholding information or giving false assurances. Employees become discouraged. Employees who are laid off may feel as if they were nameless numbers. Remaining employees feel uncomfortable and maybe even guilty because they didn't lose their jobs. Companies can avoid losing skilled personnel who might choose early retirement because of their fears for the future. The best way is to reach consensus on perceptions.

The reader will find this text difficult to follow because the key terms are missing in the body of the text. The reader must fit all the thoughts together without aid from the writer. That is a very difficult task for readers, and many will give up without finishing the document.

Repeat key terms and show how they fit with a new idea. Talk the reader through your thoughts. As you add new thoughts, each will fall into place because the key terms hold the ideas together.

The same paragraph follows, with the key terms joining the thoughts as the writer presents each thought. The key terms are bolded for this example. Notice especially that the first sentence and last sentence contain all the key terms.

When a company considers **downsizing**, good **communication between management and employees** is very important. **Communication** helps **employees** understand the reasons for the **downsizing**, reducing their feelings of insecurity and rejection. Often, **management communicates** unclearly and tries to hide the actual dimension of the **downsizing** by withholding information or giving false assurances. **Employees** become discouraged because of the lack of **communication**. **Employees** who are laid off during the **downsizing** may feel as if they were nameless numbers. Remaining **employees** feel uncomfortable and maybe even guilty because they didn't lose their jobs, but haven't received the **communication** from **management** to help them understand why.

Companies can avoid losing skilled **employees** who might choose early retirement because lack of **communication** about the **downsizing** has increased their fears for the future. The best way to keep **employees** is to reach an understanding between **management** and **employees** about the **downsizing** through clear **communication**.

Best Practice

Fully explain the concept behind every new
key term as the reader encounters it.

Guidelines for this best practice:

1. Define and connect the key terms.

2. Avoid writing strings of concepts.

The concepts in explicit documents build on one another to form a cohesive message in readers' minds. The key terms present the concepts. Each key term is like a cell in a spreadsheet. For readers to have an accurate total understanding after finishing your document, they must understand the concept in every key term, just as the number in every cell of a spreadsheet must be accurate to result in a correct total.

If readers do not understand one key term, the conclusion they come to may be inaccurate.

As a result, watch for new key terms when you first write them. **Define** every new key term if you are not sure the reader will understand it. You don't have to define it every time you use it, but you must be certain that the reader knows its meaning each time you use it. Then **connect** every new concept with the previous concepts. Don't go on until you are sure the reader will understand how the new key term fits into the big picture. Build your message very carefully so that at the end of it, the reader comes to the conclusions you want.

❖ Example

The sample that follows introduces new concepts without defining them or connecting them. You can analyze the sample by locating each key term representing a concept and looking for the definition and connection. Since the heading is "The Creative Briefing Process," the reader will expect to see the key term, "creative briefing process," in the text.

The Creative Briefing Process

Clients employ our advertising company to solve brand problems and exploit brand opportunities. That requires a functional instrument designed to achieve specific objectives. A very important part of the advertising campaign is the information that we present to the client to help the client make decisions about the advertising. The creative brief is an introduction to the advertising plan. The creative team and the client use the process to make sure the client is in on the planning and has ownership of the design.

You probably found this paragraph difficult to follow because the writer does not define new key terms and does not connect them to the preceding key terms. The title uses the key term "creative briefing process," but that doesn't appear in the paragraph. Instead, "creative brief" and "process" appear separately.

❖ Rewritten version

Notice in this rewritten version that the information contains the key terms, defined and connected. The writer defines "creative briefing" and "process" in the first paragraph and then uses those key terms throughout the second paragraph. They are key terms that unify the message. The words are bolded for this illustration:

The Creative Briefing Process

Clients use our advertising company to develop advertising campaigns that solve brand problems and exploit brand opportunities. We present our plans for the advertising campaigns in **creative briefs.** The **creative brief** is a description of the types of advertisements, their placement, and the process by which we will create them. We call the activity of producing the **creative brief** the **creative briefing process.** The goal of the **creative briefing process** is to ensure a successful marketing campaign.

We involve the client in the **creative briefing process** so the client is in on the planning and has ownership of it. In this **process**, the creative team and the client discuss the parts of the **creative brief** to be sure everyone agrees the advertising campaign will accomplish the client's goals of solving the brand problems or exploiting the brand opportunities.

In your own documents, track the key terms to make sure you have defined and connected every key concept. The key concepts represented by the key terms in the introduction should appear throughout the explanation and be repeated in the last sentence.

Follow these guidelines each time you use a new key term:

1. Decide whether the key term begins a new thought. If it does, make that apparent to the reader by breaking for a new paragraph and adding a transition ("Another," "In addition," "On the other hand").

2. Be sure the reader knows the definition of every new key term. You don't have to define it if you are confident the reader knows its definition, but you must be certain that the reader knows it before you introduce more information. If the reader needs to know something that appears later on the page to understand the key term, you must reorganize the page so everything the

reader needs to understand fully the key term either precedes the key term or is in the definition accompanying it.

3. Be sure the reader knows how the concept in the new key term connects to the concepts you've just presented and to the central idea. If you have doubts, explain the connection clearly. Don't introduce a new key term until you are sure the current one has firm connections.

Avoid writing strings of concepts.

Writers who don't know their subject well or don't understand the relationships among the concepts in the subject write strings of concepts using one new key term after another without defining the concepts or connecting them to other concepts already presented. The strings of new key terms give readers the impression the writer is rambling.

❖ Example

> Having enough ball bearings in stock is a critical action. Inventory records sometimes don't show all the items we have. Systems have limitations from the storage capacities. Creating columns with enough size is essential to take care of the problem.

Readers will find themselves hopelessly lost in four short sentences. The writer begins with the key term, "having enough ball bearings," then introduces more key terms ("inventory records" and "don't show all the items we have") without explaining how those concepts fit with "having enough ball bearings." The writer adds "systems have limitations from the storage capacities," "inventory records sometimes don't show all the items we have," and "creating columns with enough size." The reader is left bewildered. The writer has presented unexplained concepts and added other unexplained concepts, increasing the reader's confusion.

To ensure that the reader can understand and follow your message, use the key terms as your guides. Each time you introduce a new key term, think about whether the reader will know how it fits with the concepts in previous key terms and with the central idea key terms. If you have doubts, explain the relationships again.

Always err on the side of being too clear. What follows is the text about ball bearings with the key terms defined and connected. The key terms are bolded for this illustration:

We must have enough **ball bearings** in stock to avoid running short. **Inventory records** sometimes don't show all the items we have, so we may believe we have enough **ball bearings** but end up running short because the **records** showed more than we actually have. The reason the **inventory records** have errors is that we created shortened **fields** so the entries would take up less storage space, but sometimes the **fields** don't accept the inventory numbers. To avoid this problem in the future, we must create **fields** large enough to store accurate **inventory** numbers so the **records** show the number of **ball bearings** we actually have.

The writer has defined and connected the concepts using the same key terms throughout. Transition words show how each idea fits with the others. When the writer introduces the key term "fields," she defines the key term and then uses it consistently.

If you define the key terms and explain the connections clearly, the organization will follow naturally.

Best Practice

Have a clear focus for the entire document and for each block in the document.

Explicit business writing limits the message to the core points the reader must know to achieve the objectives, with no irrelevant information. Each block must focus on a single concept.

Use the key terms to make sure your message is focused. The key terms you use in the opening should appear consistently throughout the explanation. Do not add new key terms in the explanation that are not relevant to those in the opening.

❖ Example

You will find the following paragraph difficult to follow. When you track the key terms, you will see that the writer has included irrelevant information and has omitted some information that was promised in the opening sentence. The opening sentence promises this paragraph will be about three functions that consulting firm accounting systems perform: time tracking, billing, and collections. The key terms are bolded:

> **Consulting firms** today must find **accounting systems** to perform the basic functions that keep the firm in business: **time tracking, billing,** and **collections.** The system must track consulting **time by location, client, and project.** Firms with **offices spread throughout the world** need a system that can accommodate not only a number of **locations, companies, and currencies** but **different languages** as well. Firms also must have systems that provide **collection modules** capable of **automated identification, tracking, and collection of outstanding accounts receivables.**

As you track the key terms, you find that two of the key terms used in the introduction ("time tracking" and "collections") appear in the paragraph. That shows that the writer did follow through with explaining those concepts. However, a new key term ("offices spread throughout the world") appears, and the key term, "billing," presented in the opening does not appear again in the paragraph. That tells you that the writer added a concept in the explanation and excluded one that should have been explained.

Follow this process to use key terms to evaluate the focus of your document:

1. Identify the key terms in the opening sentences.

2. Look for the same key terms in the explanation, in the same order. If any do not appear, then you may have omitted a topic.

3. Look for any key terms you did not specify in the opening. If you find any, they should clearly add detail for one of the key terms you listed in the opening. In the example above, "collection modules" has three key terms adding detail about it: "automated identification, tracking, and collection of outstanding accounts receivables." Those new key terms are appropriate for the paragraph.

If you find new key terms that don't directly support one of the key terms you listed in the opening, decide whether they are new topics that you should delete, or whether you should relocate them to another place in the document.

Present concept explanations together.

Keep explanations of a concept together. As you check your document's organization, identify the key term that is the focus of each block. Use that as the name for the block to help you maintain focus. Examine the block to ensure that the key term appears and that no other key terms intrude unless they are clearly related to the key term that is the focus of the block. If you see a key term that is the focus of a block appearing in another block, it could mean you need to put the information about that key term's concept into just one block.

❖ Example

This example is confusing because the explanations of the concepts are not kept together. The key term "motors" appears in two places. The key terms are bolded for this illustration.

We need to change the way we **monitor** our **inventory** so we don't run out of **components**. We'll need enough **motors** tested and ready to install to keep going even if our supplier runs out again. We also will run through 250 unit **doors** in two days, meaning we really should have at least 500 **doors** in inventory at any time. In addition, we need enough unit **casings** to have 250 in enamel, 250 drying, and 250 ready to use.

If we run out of **motors**, our production stops. The line should have 250 **motors** ready for assembly at any time to keep the process from stopping even if our supplier runs out again. That requires that we test them and have them on the shelf.

The author is writing as she thinks. When we look at the key terms, we find the key term "motors" in the first sentence of the first paragraph, then the key terms "doors" and "unit casings," showing that the focus has shifted to doors, then to unit casings. In the second paragraph, the key term "motors" appears again. The writer should have maintained the focus for each block by naming each using a key term and using the name to ensure that each block presented all the information about the topic. The first block should be the "motors" block. The second block should be the "doors" block. A third block should be the "unit casings" block.

The following revision of the information has three blocks, one for each of the three key terms: "motors," "doors," and "casings." The opening sentence lists the key terms and eliminates "components" because that key term is not used again in the document.

We need to change the way we **monitor** our **inventory** so we don't run out of **motors, doors,** and **casings.**

We must have enough **motors** tested and ready to install to keep the process from stopping even if our supplier runs out again. If we run out of **motors,** our production stops. The line should have 250 **motors** ready for assembly at any time. That requires that we test them and have them on the shelf.

We also will run through 250 unit **doors** in two days, meaning we really should have at least 500 **doors** in inventory at any time.

Finally, we need enough unit **casings** to have 250 in enamel, 250 drying, and 250 ready to use.

Notice that the writer uses one-sentence paragraphs. They are perfectly acceptable in explicit business writing to keep concepts in clearly separated blocks.

The text would be even easier to follow if the writer broke out the list into numbered or bulleted points:

We need to change the way we monitor our inventory so we don't run out of motors, doors, and casings.

- We must have enough motors tested and ready to install to keep the process from stopping even if our supplier runs out again. If we run out of motors, our production stops. The line should have 250 motors ready for assembly at any time. That requires that we test them and have them on the shelf.

- We also will run through 250 unit doors in two days, meaning we really should have at least 500 doors in inventory at any time.

- Finally, we need enough unit casings to have 250 in enamel, 250 drying, and 250 ready to use.

The writing will be even more explicit if the writer breaks out the list using a bolded key term as a heading for each block and white space to separate the blocks, as in this example:

We need to change the way we monitor our inventory so we don't run out of motors, doors, and casings.

Motors   We must have enough motors tested and ready to install to keep the process from stopping even if our supplier runs out again. If we run out of motors, our production stops. The line should have 250 motors ready for assembly at any time. That requires that we test them and have them on the shelf.

Doors   We also will run through 250 unit doors in two days, meaning we really should have at least 500 doors in inventory at any time.

Casings   Finally, we need enough unit casings to have 250 in enamel, 250 drying, and 250 ready to use.

Best Practice

Communicate technical subjects clearly to non-technical readers.

Guidelines for this best practice:

1. Understand what the non-technical reader wants and needs.

2. Don't oversimplify the information.

3. Use clear, simple vocabulary.

4. Minimize use of abbreviations and acronyms.

5. Use a helpful tone.

6. Format the presentation to make it easy to read.

7. Use presentation strategies when you must write for both technical and non-technical readers.

The key to writing explanations of technical subjects for non-technical readers is to write everyday words in place of the technical, jargon words. You will find it easier to replace technical concepts with concepts that readers know when you focus on changing the technical, jargon words to plain, simple words.

Become familiar with your non-technical readers:

1. Know the vocabulary in your area of expertise that each group of your readers understands.

2. Have carefully developed evaluations of the readers' knowledge of the subject, educational background, technical expertise, need for concreteness, and need for depth.

3. After you give them a non-technical explanation of a technical subject, ask for feedback from them about whether they understood your explanations easily.

4. If you are part of a team that regularly writes reports for specific groups of readers, your team should come to a consensus about

the readers and prepare a set of written guidelines for the documents you write for them.

Understand what the non-technical reader wants and needs.

In the first chapter, you rated the depth the readers require:

- Little depth
- Moderate depth
- Considerable depth

Evaluate the key terms you wrote and organized in your notes to see whether they provide all the depth the reader needs but not more. Adjust your notes before going on by adding anything the reader needs and deleting anything that exceeds what the reader needs. Then write the document according to the non-technical reader's need for depth.

Little depth

- Present only the conclusions, recommendations, or brief points bulleted out or numbered.

- Use no jargon or only jargon you know this reader will understand.

Moderate depth

- Write a summary for each conclusion, recommendation, or point using everyday language.

- You will have some detail for this reader, but you must watch for the point at which you should stop adding detail. Write as little detail as you can that will still satisfy the reader's needs.

- Avoid presenting a lecture on the subject or including information you feel is very interesting but isn't necessary for the reader to know.

Considerable depth

- Since this reader does not have high technical knowledge, the reader likely will be a project director or upper-level manager who must present the information to others, but who does not have technical expertise. Provide enough detail to help this reader articulate the principles involved using plain, non-technical English at whatever level that person's listeners or readers want.

- Begin with a bulleted or numbered list of the conclusions, recommendations, or points using no jargon. Follow with the detail in the same order.

- Substitute clear, plain explanations that approach the technical understanding as much as you can, then stop. You may reach a point at which the translation into non-technical language does not permit you to explain the entire process. Summarize what happens in everyday language without explaining the detail.

In this example, the reader does not need to know the contents of the formula:

> The mixer then uses a special formula for the chemical mix that provides the precise amount of etching liquid without making it so strong it will burn too much of the plate.

General considerations for writing for a non-technical reader

- Watch for words with three or more syllables to see if you're falling into jargon or unnecessarily complex vocabulary. Try to find substitutes.

- Use short sentences. Keep your average sentence length to around 15 to 20 words. Edit wordy phrases to make them concise.

- You may teach the reader words that are important for even a non-technical person in the field to know. Teach the words by defining and explaining them the first time you use them. However, avoid teaching all the jargon.

Don't oversimplify the information.

Some business people with technical expertise object to "dumbing down" the information for non-technical readers. However, they misunderstand what it means to present technical information simply.

The explanation can be simple, but still provide all the understanding the reader needs. An explanation using clear, plain English words does not require leaving out content; it just means using words and concepts a non-technical reader can understand.

❖ Example

For example, the writer would be writing technically if he wrote this about the sun:

> The sun's energy comes from the fusion of four hydrogen nuclei, each with the mass of one proton, to form a single helium nucleus (two protons and two neutrons) that has a mass of 3.97 times the mass of one proton, giving off an amount of mass equal to 0.03 times the mass of one proton that is converted to energy equal to $0.03 \times$ (mass one proton) $\times$ c2.

The writer would be oversimplifying the content of the message if he wrote this:

> The sun is a huge furnace in which hydrogen burns up and changes into helium.

That's oversimplifying the content because the sun's energy comes from nuclear fusion, not the chemical breakdown releasing heated gases that occurs in a furnace. However, the writer could write simply but keep the integrity of the content:

> The sun is a ball of extremely hot gases heated by a continuous nuclear explosion that has gone on for 4.5 billion years. The nuclear reaction converts hydrogen to helium, giving off energy in the process.

The concepts, "hot gases," and "nuclear explosion" are common knowledge. The writer has changed the vocabulary to fit the reader's lack of technical background, but has not oversimplified the content to be distorted or untrue.

Writing about complex, technical subjects in ways that help non-technical readers understand the concepts requires a knowledgeable writer. The more knowledgeable and intelligent the writer is, the more likely she will be able to explain the subject clearly for the non-technical reader, using her depth of knowledge of the subject to create ways of presenting it without the jargon.

The less knowledgeable the writer is, the more likely she will fall into using jargon and complex phrases because she doesn't understand the concepts well enough to explain them clearly.

As you write, each time you come to a technical word or concept, find the common concept closely enough aligned with the technical subject that you can substitute as an alternative. Often the substitute will require more words. Below are some examples:

Technical concept	Common concept
Create behavioral objectives.	Specify what you want trainees to do to demonstrate they've learned the skill.
Write to a file.	Save the document.
Test whether the silicone vulcanization is complete.	Touch the silicone to see if it is no longer sticky, showing that the drying process was successful.
There was a malfunction in the multiloop controller on the POD tank.	The problem was with the device that measures temperature on the tank where the manufacturing process takes place.

Use clear, simple vocabulary.

Complex language is different from jargon, although business people sometimes confuse the two. Readers may assume that a report about a technical subject is difficult to follow because of the subject when it is actually difficult because of the complex words the writer uses. The words are not jargon words, but are words people don't commonly use in writing and speaking. Don't use unusual, complex language in any of your writing, for either technical or non-technical readers.

Some examples of complex words that have more desirable, simple alternatives follow:

Complex words	Simple words
ascertain	find out, learn
consummate	close, bring about
contextualization	put into context
definitive	precise, conclusive
domicile	home
extensible	extendable
financial deficit	losing money
incomprehensible	difficult to understand
incredulous	disbelieving
initialize	begin, start
initiate	begin, start
metamodel	system model
obfuscate	obscure
obtuse	indistinct
ostensibly	apparently
peruse	read, study
precipitate	cause
predicated	based on
presumptive	presumed
proscribe	prohibit
sanguine	reddish, cheerful
schema	diagram, model
terminate	end

The following table has examples of words that many business readers will understand, but when a simpler word is available, always choose to use it. Simple words communicate more clearly and quickly.

Complex words	Simple words
advise	tell
along the lines of	like
are of the opinion	believe
assumption	belief
commence	begin, start
despite the fact that	although, though
during the course of	during
for the purpose of	for, to
for the reason that	because
give consideration to	consider
have need for	need
in view of the fact that	because, since
it has come to my attention	[omit]
make use of	use
nevertheless	but
on the occasion of	when
preceding year	last year
prior to	before
provide assistance	help, converse, talk
regarding	about
reside	live
subsequent to	after
succeed in making	make
utilize	use
with reference to	about

Follow these guidelines for the words you use:

1. For non-technical readers, use everyday words in place of jargon.

2. Even for readers who are knowledgeable about the field, use plain, simple words for all vocabulary that is not jargon.

3. Write definitions at the points where readers need them.

    - Don't define jargon words at the beginning and expect the reader to remember them throughout. Instead, use the simpler words you would use in the definition in place of the jargon word each time you feel the need to use the jargon word.

    - Don't depend on glossaries. Many readers read on past the jargon term with faulty understanding of the text because they don't want to use the glossary. If you have a word for which you feel you need a glossary, don't use the word if possible. If it's necessary that you use it, define it in the text and consider including a short explanation for it in parentheses the first two or three times you use it.

❖ Example

Writing with unclear words and jargon	Redrafted in plain language
From any HTML file on a Web site, one can link to files through URLs that point to other HTML files in the current site or files resident in other domains on alternative servers. Specifically, these links are URLs, a unique concatenation of alphanumeric characters and symbols that are not displayed. Instead, link text is designated in the HTML as clickable, so identified through underlining and blue pixilation, which may be avoided through the utilization of cascading style sheet protocols.	You can link any page to other pages on the same site or different sites using page addresses. For example, the page address that links to our personnel directory is http://joysonco.com/personnel.html. The text normally doesn't show the page address itself. Instead, it shows a description of the content, such as "Personnel directory." The description text is normally blue and underlined to signal that when you click on the text, the page will appear.

Use a helpful tone.

When you know the subject well and are writing for a non-technical reader, it is easy to use a patronizing tone or write to the reader as though he were a child. Instead, write clear, simple explanations you would speak to an intelligent adult.

❖ Example

This non-technical explanation is patronizing.

> The program allows you to change field lengths, but unless you know what you're doing, you don't want to do that. You wouldn't try to change the wiring in your toaster, would you? The reason you shouldn't change the field lengths is too complex to explain easily here. Just don't do it.

The following explanation points out that the practice may cause problems, but doesn't imply that the reader is too ignorant to understand why:

> The program allows for changes field lengths, but it is set up to use the field lengths the programmers placed in it before providing it to you. Therefore, changing the field lengths may cause the program to function improperly. If you want to change field lengths, contact us and we'll be happy to help you.

Format the presentation to make it easy to read.

Use visuals, graphs, and tables if they present the information clearly. If they require that the reader understand the content before being able to understand the visual, don't use it. You should not simply copy the visuals from the technical document to the non-technical document. Include only tables that are clear for the non-technical reader.

Use headings to divide the parts of your document. Skip blank lines between the parts. White space helps readers navigate the explanations.

Use presentation strategies when you must write for both technical and non-technical readers.

If you must write a document for both technical and non-technical readers, use one of the following strategies explained in Chapter 4 under the heading, "When readers have differing needs or abilities, write different versions of the document or sections within the document to match the readers' needs and abilities." These are the three strategies explained there:

1. Write separate documents for readers with differing needs or abilities.

2. Write different parts for readers with differing needs or abilities.

3. Use sidebars, boxed text, and other devices on the same pages with explanations for readers with differing needs or abilities.

Best Practice

Write instructions and procedures that are complete, concrete, and clear.

Guidelines for this best practice:

1. Prepare the reader for the instructions or procedures.

2. Include all the instructions or steps the reader needs, where the reader needs them.

3. Format the actions so the reader can follow them easily.

4. Describe forms, screens, fields, and equipment parts clearly.

5. Explain choices fully.

6. Write a conclusion for the instructions that will be helpful to the reader.

The greatest problem business writers have with writing instructions and procedures is that they don't include all of the steps the reader must follow in sufficient detail for the reader to be successful. The reader needs to have all of the information necessary to complete the instructions or procedures successfully.   That requires that you include detailed instructions and explanations at the specific points where the readers need them. Follow these guidelines:

1. **Prepare the reader for the instructions or procedures.**

    - Begin the instructions or procedures with an explanation of their purpose and outcome. Be sure readers know why they are following the instructions or procedure. You may write a statement as simple as "Follow this procedure to enter customer-record information."

    - Describe all resources the reader must use. Where does the reader obtain them? How are they to be used?

    - At the beginning of the instructions, explain the timing and conditions required for the activity. By what date or time must this be completed? What conditions must be met for this to be satisfactory? What critical or special activities must be performed?

      Instead of: Get together the consultant's travel arrangements.

      Write: We will need to have the consultant's travel arrangements completed by Thursday. Get paper copies of all arrangements so we have a record of them. Make sure the consultant receives them by Friday morning.

    - Explain where the reader should be at the beginning and make sure the reader can get there. If the reader must begin at a screen in the software, state the name of the screen and make sure the reader knows how to access it.

2. **Include all the instructions the reader needs, where the reader needs them.**

    - Write all the actions the reader must perform in the order in which the reader must perform them. Do not assume the reader will know to perform an unstated action.

    - Don't refer the reader to a procedure or a definition somewhere else in the same set of instructions. Repeat the procedure or definition where the reader must use it.

- Anticipate errors. Explain how to avoid them and how to recover from them.

- If you use tables for instructions, don't let the table format limit the amount of explanation.

- Include all words in instruction sentences.

  Instead of this: Locate serial # and type in.

  Write this: Locate the serial number and type it in the field.

3. **Format the actions so the reader can follow them easily.**

- Start actions with numbers: "1" or "Step 1." Specify only one action following each number.

- Skip a blank line between actions.

- Don't assign numbers to results or explanations by themselves; write the results or explanations after the actions.

- Be careful about words that require knowledge of several actions. For example, "Select the delivery mode" assumes that the user knows what the delivery modes are, which is appropriate, and how to do the selecting. If you believe the reader may not know how to perform one of the component actions, explain it.

- Use action verbs at the beginnings of the actions ("Click . . .," "Type . . .," "Write . . .," "Fill out . . .," "Call . . ."). Prefer a concrete, sensed action rather than general term such as "Select" or "Input."

  Instead of this: Maintenance should know . . .

  Write this: Call maintenance to describe . . .

  Instead of this: Select the binding type.

  Write this: Click on the circle beside the binding type.

4. **Describe forms, screens, fields, and equipment parts clearly.**

- For fields on a form or screen, describe the location and name for the field, with uppercase and lowercase letters exactly as they appear on the form or screen.

- For keys on the keyboard, write the name as it appears on the keyboard and end with "key" (Esc key, Ctrl key). You might use the convention of putting the key name in brackets: "the [Esc] key."

- When possible and appropriate, include a screen image, cross-section, sample form, equipment diagram, or other visual. Use callouts or boxes to pinpoint the areas you are referencing.

- Define any words, such as field names, with which the reader may not be familiar.

5. **Explain choices fully.**

- Explain choice options fully at the point at which the reader must make the choice. Don't assume the reader will remember an explanation presented earlier in the document.

- When the reader must make a choice, state the conditions and explain the options. Separate them clearly.

  Example:

  Type one of the following for the amount:

  | If . . . | it is **negative** | type the amount in the "Loss" field. |
  | | it is **positive** | type the amount in the "Profit" field. |

6. **Write a conclusion for the instructions that will be helpful to the reader.**

- End with a description of the ending state, such as the screen the reader will come to, message that will appear, or response the reader will receive, as in these examples:

  You will see the main data entry screen again.

  Within three days, you will receive a confirmation of your travel reservations in an e-mail.

- Provide contact information for someone the reader can contact if there is a problem. If the procedure is critical, ask the reader to contact you after the first successful completion.

❖ Example of a step-by-step procedure

This step-by-step procedure includes all the necessary details for the user to be successful. It is formatted so actions follow numbers or "Step" designations. The results (what the reader sees) follow the actions.

Hello Lacy,

You asked for the procedure your staff can use to install Sound Booster. The procedure follows:

Task 1: Prepare the system to use Sound Booster.

Start the Sound Manager program as you normally do. You will see the opening menu with "Sound Manager" at the top.

Step 1. Click on the third option: "Set up Sound Booster." You will see the "Set up Sound Booster Options" screen.

Action   *Result (what the reader sees)*

Step 2. Follow this process to set up Sound Booster:

1. In the list of "Sound Booster types," click on the button beside the Sound Booster hardware you have. The cursor will jump to the "Computer types" field after you click on the button.

2. In the list of "Computer types," click on the button next to your computer type. The cursor will jump to the "Serial number" field.

3. Type the serial number for your Sound Booster software. It is on the registration card at the bottom of the first page.

4. Press the [Enter] key. A box will appear around the "OK" button.

5. Click on "OK." You will see a screen with "Modem Settings" at the top. The procedures that follow explain how to set up the modem.

Task 2: Set up your modem.

[explanation continues here]

❖ Example of instructions

TO: All Managers

FROM: Director of Facilities Management

SUBJECT: Scheduling rooms for meetings. DO IT EARLY.

Introduction   As our fall projects that we have taken on move toward completion, we are receiving more requests for room usage.

Marge, the facilities manager, coordinates room usage so everyone can use rooms freely without conflicts in scheduling.

Contents   This memorandum explains the following:

1. The instructions for booking a room

2. Facilities Management's policy for room bookings and usage that will help you as you plan your meetings

---

Instructions for booking a room

Step	Action
1	Call Marge as soon as you know you will be holding a meeting to check on availability.
2	Obtain a blank Form 3482, Room Reservation Request, from Facilities Planning and fill it out as explained in the next steps.
3	**If you need special equipment . . .** Discuss your needs with the manager as soon as you know of them to make sure what you need is available. In the "Equipment needed" blank, specify the special equipment you need such as workstations or the LCD projector.

	If you need no special equipment . . . State that you have no equipment needs on the form in the "Equipment needed" blank so the facilities coordinator does not contact you to see if you need anything.
4	**If you want amenities . . .** Specify the amenities you want in the "Amenities?" blank. Coffee will be provided unless you specify that you do not want it. **If you have no amenities needs . . .** Specify that you want no amenities in the "Amenities?" blank. Coffee will still be provided for you unless you specify that you do not want coffee.
5	At the bottom of the Form 3482, fill out the special instructions portion to let us know whether you need a technician to set up electronic equipment or access to the Internet on workstations. Be brief.
6	When you finish the form, make a photocopy of your Form 3482 worksheet so the facilities coordinator can see the details about what you need. Attach it to the blue copy of your Form 3482 that you send to facilities management.

7	**File this copy:**	**In:**
	blue	Facilities Management office
	pink	your department file
	yellow	your own records

Policy for room bookings and usage   [memo continues here]

As with all explicit business writing, the format identifying the blocks enhances the clear, straightforward text. Formatting and text together make the writing so clear it cannot be misunderstood.

Best Practice

Provide sufficient, relevant evidence for statements.

Guidelines for this best practice:

1. Identify the conclusions in your writing.
2. State the conclusion.
3. Prove the conclusion.
4. At times, present the facts, then the conclusion.
5. Prefer complete, verifiable facts.
6. Avoid including inconsequential facts.
7. Avoid teaching and preaching.
8. Avoid patronizing, insinuating, castigating, and lecturing.
9. Format the facts so they are easy to follow.

Explicit documents state conclusions and the evidence that led to the conclusions to increase the likelihood that the reader will agree with the conclusions and respond as expected.

Identify the conclusions in your writing.

When you prepared your notes for the document, you wrote key terms at Level 1, Level 2, and so on. Some of those key terms are facts, such as the time for a meeting, the server on which the software resides, and the percentage of focus group participants who said they didn't like comparing your product to a flower in bloom. Others are conclusions that are not themselves facts, but that you believe are true because two or more facts support the statement: the conclusion that we should not hold the meetings on Mondays, the conclusion that server A is better suited to the software than server B, and the conclusion that we shouldn't compare our product to a flower.

❖ Example

In this report, the conclusions are bolded. The remaining text contains facts supporting the conclusions.

> Today's customers are progressively more Internet-savvy, so **it's increasingly likely that many of them are (or will be) reaching out to you via e-mail.** In fact, e-mail and Web-based communications are growing faster than any other means of customer interaction.
>
> As a result, **managing e-mail effectively is critical to your organization's ability to service customers.** The customers of today are increasingly familiar with your competitors and are no longer willing to wait for you to get back to them. From the moment an e-mail-based customer inquiry reaches your company, the clock is ticking. You must have the capacity to answer customer inquiries quickly, despite potentially high volumes of e-mail, answer customer inquiries accurately with information relevant to the customer's needs, and use e-mail to build lasting relationships with your customers.

These are the conclusions with the facts that support them.

CONCLUSION:	It's increasingly likely that many of [today's customers] are (or will be) reaching out to you via e-mail. **Why do I say that? Here's why:**
	FACT 1: Today's customers are progressively more Internet-savvy,
	FACT 2: In fact, e-mail and Web-based communications are growing faster than any other means of customer interaction.
CONCLUSION:	Managing e-mail effectively is critical to your organization's ability to service customers. **Why do I say that? Here's why:**
	FACT 1: The customers of today are increasingly familiar with your competitors and are no longer willing to wait for you to get back to them.

> FACT 2: From the moment an e-mail-based customer inquiry reaches your company, the clock is ticking.
>
> FACT 3: You must have the capacity to answer customer inquiries quickly, despite potentially high volumes of e-mail.
>
> FACT 4: You must have the capacity to answer customer inquiries accurately.
>
> FACT 5: You must have the capacity to answer customer inquiries with information relevant to the customer's needs.
>
> FACT 6: You must have the capacity to build lasting relationships with your customers.

The writer states a conclusion, then proves the conclusion.

State your conclusion.

Identify the conclusions in your key terms. When you write your explanation, state the conclusion at the beginning or close to the beginning of the block of text.

Prove your conclusion.

Now, look at the key terms for the information that will justify your conclusion to the reader. Decide how many facts to include based on your objectives and your analysis of the readers. Explain each fact clearly and completely enough that the reader will understand why you came to the conclusion. When you've proven the conclusion sufficiently, stop.

At times, present the facts, then the conclusion.

At times, you will need to explain the facts and then state the conclusion, but that isn't normally the best order. If the reader knows the conclusion first, he will be attuned to hearing the facts and putting them into place. If you explain the facts before explaining the conclusion, the reader has to keep the facts in mind without knowing where you're going and then put them all into place after you finally state the conclusion.

❖ Example

An example of putting the conclusion after the facts follows. The conclusion is bolded. The facts are in the remaining text.

Parts are obsolete for our old Hemming 250 rig. It has been down several times this past year and we can expect more breakdowns and increased repair costs if we keep using it. We can't buy the Protal A50 because it exceeds the allowable noise levels set by MSHA. **We should go ahead and purchase the BOS 25 auger rig for sand and gravel drilling.**

The reader would have to read the facts in the first sentences not knowing where the writer is going, then reread the paragraph after reading the conclusion at the end to see whether the facts justified the conclusion.

This is the same text with the conclusion at the beginning. Knowing the conclusion before reading the facts allows the reader to put the facts into context.

We should go ahead and purchase the BOS 25 auger rig for sand and gravel drilling. Parts are obsolete for our old Hemming 250 rig. It has been down several times this past year and we can expect more breakdowns and increased repair costs if we keep using it. We can't buy the Protal A50 because it exceeds the allowable noise levels set by MSHA.

Always prefer to state the conclusion, then the facts. State the point; then prove the point.

The more explicit way to present the conclusion and facts is to introduce them and break them out into a numbered list:

We should go ahead and purchase the BOS 25 auger rig for sand and gravel drilling for three reasons:

1. Parts are obsolete for our old Hemming 250 rig.

2. It has been down several times this past year and we can expect more breakdowns and increased repair costs if we keep using it.

3. We can't buy the Protal A50 because it exceeds the allowable noise levels set by MSHA.

Provide complete, verifiable facts.

Present the strongest facts first. Provide sources and data as necessary to make the case that brought you to your conclusion. The reader may not agree with you, but should understand how you arrived at your conclusion.

Anticipate questions and disagreements from your readers. Provide a clear explanation of why those questions or disagreements are not relevant or not true. Be careful to limit these explanations that you make in anticipation; you can overdo it by raising issues that would not occur to the reader.

Avoid being redundant. State the fact once and then go on to the next fact. Repeating the facts using different words is usually not helpful.

❖ Example

In the following example, the writer repeats the facts unnecessarily, hoping that repeating them will give them more weight. However, explaining the points twice just adds unnecessary text and increases the possibility for confusion.

> When a problem with computer software creates a disaster, the failure is often blamed on bad programming. However, the cause is usually the result of poor management, communication, or training. It most often isn't a programming error. **The software programming is blamed, but most often the operator's actions weren't managed properly, the operator wasn't informed about something pertaining to the operation, or the operator wasn't trained properly to use the software.**

When the writer repeats the ideas, the reader has to reread both statements to see whether the writer has listed six points or just three points twice. In this example, the repeated facts are clearer than the original because they add explanation. The writer should delete the original statement ("the cause is usually the result of poor management, communication, or training") and keep the more detailed statement.

Avoid including inconsequential facts.

Some facts may seem to add to the conclusion's strength, but they may be weak facts. If you have a sufficient number of facts other than the weak fact, avoid including it. Using inconsequential or irrelevant evidence weakens your conclusion and wastes readers' time. The reader can also get stuck on the weak facts, missing or trivializing your point.

You may feel strongly about the subject or be greatly engrossed in it, but the reader should receive only the information that he needs and wants. You must stay focused on the reader as you write. Delete irrelevant facts.

❖ Example

In the following example, the writer wants to emphasize the point that the problem with software failures is most often not the programming, but she adds a fact that is weak and detracts from the stronger statement. The weak fact is bolded.

> When a problem with computer software creates a disaster, the failure is often blamed on bad programming. However, the cause is most often that the operator's actions weren't managed properly, the operator wasn't informed about something pertaining to the operation, or the operator wasn't trained properly to use the software. **Programmers are trained to take great care in debugging software to create an error-free product, so they rarely create bad software.**

The writer has already established that programming most often doesn't cause the problem. Adding the note about programmers being conscientious in their programming adds nothing of value to the writer's explanation and the reader's understanding.

Format the facts so they are easy to follow

When possible, break out the facts into a numbered or bulleted list using one number or bullet for each fact. The numbered or bulleted list makes the facts easier to read and gives them emphasis.

The clearest introduction to the facts is an explicit statement: "We have come to that conclusion for three reasons" or "These six facts brought us to make these recommendations." If you simply start explaining the facts without an introduction to them, be sure the reader knows you are starting the facts, not presenting a new conclusion.

❖ Example

In the following example, the writer breaks out the list to make it clearer and give it emphasis. The list is preceded by an explicit introduction that states the exact number of items in the list:

When a problem with computer software creates a disaster, the failure is often blamed on bad programming. However, the failure is most often caused by one of these three problems:

1. The operator's actions weren't managed properly.

2. The operator wasn't informed about something pertaining to the operation.

3. The operator wasn't trained properly to use the software.

Chapter 9

Explicit business writing has clear, concise paragraphs, sentences, and words.

The building blocks of explicit business writing are paragraphs, sentences, and words. Precise words, in explicit sentences, combined into well developed paragraphs carry the reader through the writer's message. Just as a spreadsheet with all the correct figures in all the right cells results in the correct totals, carefully written paragraphs, sentences, and words bring the reader to the writer's conclusions without communication errors.

This chapter explains the best practices for writing clear, concise paragraphs, sentences, and words.

Best Practice

Write concisely.

Guidelines for this best practice:

1. Eliminate deadwood: words that convey no useful information.

2. Eliminate redundancies: words and sentences that repeat information unnecessarily.

3. Don't write the obvious.

4. Eliminate word combinations that contain redundancies or deadwood.

Explicit business writing contains core points presented in concise explanations. The more words in a sentence, the more likely it is that readers will forget or distort the meanings of some part of the sentence. Also, readers become mentally fatigued and bored with wordy text. Reading words, interpreting their meanings, and combining the words to form a whole message require time and energy.

The following paragraph contains too many words for the message:

The first main prevention method that can help our company eliminate employee theft is to perform pre-employment screening of all applicants for positions with our company. This can be a major aid to our company. Which screening technique used in the hiring process is a very important decision because it will either decrease the amount of theft or even increase it if we are not careful in hiring. We need to hire applicants for positions who have the proper work skills required for the positions and for being successful in the jobs, and applicants who have job-related values in areas such as integrity, service, and safety to ensure that there is less chance that they will engage in employee theft. To ensure this, we need to use pre-employment screening techniques that identify job candidates who possess the qualities of integrity, service, and safety, as demonstrated in their past job performance.

The same message is restated here in this single, short sentence:

> The first method of eliminating employee theft in our company is to screen applicants so we hire candidates who have the required work skills, integrity, service orientation, and concern for safety.

All of the words eliminated from the longer paragraph were redundant or unnecessary. The original paragraph about employee theft contains 150 words. The revised sentence contains 31 words, an 80 percent reduction. That reduces the writer's time in preparing the message by 80 percent. It also requires 80 percent less reader time and results in 80 percent fewer opportunities for confusion. Imagine how wonderful it would be if some of the dry, confusing manuals, e-mails, memos, letters, or reports we all receive were reduced by 80 percent. A 95-page manual would become 19 pages.

Some business writers, upon first learning the explicit business style described in this book, feel that being so clear, direct, and succinct takes the humanity out of their writing. That isn't true. The humanity is in what you say, not in the number of words you use.

Eliminate deadwood: words that convey no useful information.

Unnecessary words are deadwood. Eliminating them will not affect the information in the message, but will reduce the time and energy readers must expend to interpret the information. Here is the paragraph about employee theft with deadwood words crossed out:

The first ~~main prevention~~ method that can help our company eliminate employee theft is ~~to perform~~ pre-employment screening ~~of all applicants for positions with our company. This can be a major aid to our company. Which screening technique used in the hiring process is a very important decision because it will either decrease the amount of theft or even increase it if we are not careful in hiring. We need~~ to hire applicants ~~for positions~~ who have the proper work skills ~~required for the positions and~~ for being successful ~~in the jobs,~~ and ~~applicants who have job-related values in areas such as~~ integrity, service, and safety ~~to ensure that there is less chance that they will engage in employee theft. To ensure this, we need to use pre-employment screening techniques that identify job candidates who possess the qualities of integrity, service, and safety, as demonstrated in their past job performance.~~

Eliminate redundancies: words and sentences that repeat information unnecessarily.

Business writers often write the same thing twice, changing the wording so the second iteration sounds like new information, but it actually isn't. This description of the contents of *The Courageous Follower: Standing up to and for Our Leaders*, by Ira Chaleff (Berrett-Koehler, San Francisco, 2003) contains redundancies:

Courage is one characteristic a follower must possess to help the organization achieve its goals. More specifically, a successful follower who helps achieve organization goals must have the courage to assume responsibility, serve, challenge, participate in transformation, and leave. These are five activities that a follower must be able to perform.

The redundancies have been crossed out of this version of the paragraph:

> ~~Courage is one characteristic a follower must possess~~ to help the organization achieve its goals. ~~More specifically,~~ a successful follower ~~who helps achieve organization goals~~ must have the courage to assume responsibility, serve, challenge, participate in transformation, and leave if necessary. ~~These are five activities that a follower must be able to perform.~~

This is the same paragraph, written without the redundancies:

> To help the organization achieve its goals, a successful follower must have the courage to assume responsibility, serve, challenge, participate in transformation, and leave if necessary.

Here is another paragraph containing redundancies:

> Since the year 1990, our company has experienced real growth from a well-designed marketing program. The marketing program has resulted in an expansion in three critical areas. It resulted in the development of new products, increases in sales, and the hiring of six new employees.

The writer did not need "the year" because 1990 is obviously a year. Likewise, "experienced real growth" is the same as both "expansion" and "new products, increases in sales, and the hiring of six new employees." The writer should have combined the sentences to keep the meaning while eliminating the redundant statements:

> Since 1990, the marketing program has resulted in the development of new products, increases in sales, and hiring six new employees.

Streamline your writing by combining sentences. Your objective isn't to make the writing shorter, but that will happen. By reducing the number of words and sentences, you help the reader understand more easily, and you eliminate words that can lead to confusion.

Duplets and triplets

Duplets are two words joined by "and" that mean essentially the same thing:

> We have to act quickly and speedily.

A triplet consists of three words or phrases that mean the same thing:

> The committee decided to encourage cooperation, partnering, and working together.

Legal writing, especially, is filled with duplets, triplets, and worse:

> This contract supersedes all rules, regulations, bylaws, standards, acts, edicts, statues, codes, legislations, and all other such that existed prior to the aforementioned day and date appearing on this agreement and contract.

When you use two or more words joined by "and," check to be sure that you are not repeating ideas using different words.

Don't write the obvious.

This paragraph states the obvious, repeatedly:

> Moving the Graphics Department to the other building will result in more space for Accounting. Expanding the size of Accounting employee work areas will give them more room in which to work. That will mean more room for their workstations, supplies, and all of the tools office workers need to use to perform their jobs successfully. A larger work area will make working more pleasant for them. I propose that we expand the size of Accounting's work areas.

The author is wasting the reader's time. It is much too obvious that "expanding the size of employee work areas will give them more room in which to work." Obviously, if they have more room, the added space will be for their workstations, supplies, and other tools, and obviously, if they have a larger work area, working will be more pleasant.

Here is the message without stating the obvious:

> Moving the Graphics Department to the other building will result in more space for Accounting. I propose that we expand the size of the Accounting staff's work areas.

Readers don't mind if the writer occasionally states the obvious, but some writers fill their business documents with such statements, as in this example:

> Our company is losing money every year from inaccurate data being entered into systems and copied from one database to another, and management is very unhappy about the problem. That money could be put to use in expanding the company or attracting qualified workers or a hundred other worthwhile activities. Any other expenditure would be better than losing money due to inaccurate data. Inaccurate data is simply a matter of error somewhere in the system. Data is entered, stored, and copied to other databases, and somewhere along the way someone has done something to make the data inaccurate. This report contains a proposal for eliminating data-entry errors.

All of the text after "one database to another" is so obvious it just occupies space and requires the reader to wade through a morass of words to find the meaning. Of course management is unhappy with the problem; of course the money could be used elsewhere; of course inaccurate data results from someone's error someplace.

Here is the same paragraph with the obvious deleted:

> Our company is losing money from inaccurate data being entered into systems and copied from one database to another. This report contains a proposal for eliminating data-entry errors.

Review your writing to be sure you aren't writing information so obvious it isn't worth the space it takes up.

Eliminate word combinations that contain redundancies or deadwood.

Some word combinations commonly used in business writing contain at least one word that is redundant or deadwood. Reduce these combinations to the shorter forms:

Phrases with deadwood	Shorter forms
8:00 a.m. in the morning	8:00 a.m.
advanced ahead	advanced

at this point in time	now
basic fundamentals	fundamentals
both together	both
brief in duration	brief
bring to a resolution	resolve
bring to an end	end
consensus of opinion	consensus
cooperate together	cooperate
do a study	study
each and every	every
enclosed herein	enclosed
exactly the same	exactly
for the month of July	for July
for the purpose of	to
for the sum of	for
give a promotion	promote
give a response	respond
have a tendency to	tend
have an ability to	can
hold a conference	confer
hold a meeting	meet
hopeful optimism	optimism
important essentials	essentials
in order to	to
in the event that	if
irregardless	regardless
just exactly	exactly
located on, located in	on, in

make a decision	decide
make a recommendation	recommend
make changes in	change
make progress toward	progress toward
make reductions	reduce
merge together	merge
mutual cooperation	cooperation
on a daily basis	daily
on a monthly basis	monthly
on a yearly basis	yearly
on the occasion of	when
plan in advance	plan
prior to the start of	before
provide a summary of	summarize
reduce down	reduce
resume again	resume
seems apparent	seems
still continue	continue
take action	act
take into consideration	consider
true facts	facts
ultimate end	end
until such time as	when
write down	write

Best Practice

Write clear, focused, organized paragraphs
that help readers identify, understand, and
remember concepts.

Guidelines for this best practice:

1. Generally, keep paragraphs short.

2. Make sure the change in thought is clear to the reader.

3. Include only one idea in each paragraph, or show the clear development from one idea to another.

Explicit business writing uses paragraphs to help readers see blocks of ideas. A paragraph is marked with a blank line or blank characters before the block of text. The blank space signals to the reader that a thought has ended and another is beginning.

Paragraphs help readers shift their thinking as they read. However, readers must know the direction of the change in thought. To communicate the change clearly, open most new paragraphs with a statement explaining the shift. This sentence is called a topic sentence.

Use the same guidelines for paragraphs that you do for other blocks: connect and define. **Connect** the concept to preceding concepts. **Define** the concept within the paragraph.

Generally, keep paragraphs short.

When you start a new thought, break for a new paragraph regardless of the number of lines or sentences in the paragraphs. E-mails, letters, and memos should normally have paragraphs averaging around five lines. Try not to go beyond five lines and rarely go to seven or more lines. Reports should have paragraphs averaging seven lines, but a small number of paragraphs may as long as ten or twelve lines. This paragraph, for example, has seven lines and five sentences.

The easiest way to adjust paragraph length is to write the paragraph, then look at it to see how long it is. When it is longer than five lines in an e-mail, letter, or memo, or longer than seven lines in a report, look for a change in thought to be sure you're creating clear blocks of information.

Don't try to make all paragraphs five lines or seven lines. Use the length as a guideline to look for changes in thought. An average of five or seven lines means some paragraphs may occupy one line and some may even have ten lines.

However, if the sentences belong together to maintain the focus on a thought, use as many lines as are necessary for the paragraph. Try not to have several long paragraphs in a document. That shows that you aren't identifying changes in thought, and it will make the text too dense.

Don't be afraid of one-sentence paragraphs. They are appropriate for business documents. However, if you have a series of one-sentence paragraphs, the paragraphs won't help the reader organize the thoughts and the text will seem disjointed.

Make sure the change in thought is clear to the reader.

Always make sure the change in thought is clear to the reader. The most important way to make the change in thought clear is to examine the key term from the previous thought and key term from the next thought. Think of the key terms as the threads that hold the fabric of your business writing together.

Use one of these devices at the beginning of the paragraph:

- **First choice.** If there is a major change in thought, write a statement at the beginning of the paragraph explaining the change in thought. Include the key term that connects the new thought to the previous one or the central idea. The key terms are bolded in these statements for this illustration:

  Another **reason for the decrease in revenue** is . . .

  These **qualities in a manager** are not as important as . . .

- **Second choice:** If the change is too obvious for a statement, try to include a transition that makes the change in thought clear.

  In addition, the new building will . . .

  However, we will still need to consider . . .

Without the transition, the reader would have to guess at the relationships between your points or read all the text to figure out the relationship. In explicit business writing, never require the reader to put the pieces together on her own; present the entire picture already assembled.

Include only one idea in each paragraph, or show the clear development from one idea to another.

Limit paragraphs to one idea. When you seem to be changing ideas, decide whether the next idea fits in the same paragraph with the previous idea. If the reader needs to see the ideas as a close unit, or you are developing the paragraph from the opening concept to a conclusion, you may keep them together. Otherwise, if a new idea is clearly different, break for a new paragraph to separate the ideas.

As you evaluate your paragraphs, name each using the key term that states the central thought. That key term should appear near the beginning. If you see more than one idea in the key terms that appear in the paragraph, decide whether you have two concepts that you should separate.

❖ Example

The following paragraph is too long. The writer should look at the key terms to see where it can be broken into smaller blocks. The key term for the paragraph is "office/clerical has been the fastest growing sector." The key terms for the thoughts that follow are bolded. You will see the natural places to make new paragraphs because they are at the points where new key terms appear.

During the past 40 years, the **office/clerical sector** has been the **fastest growing sector** in the marketplace. That occurred in spite of a slowdown in growth the office/clerical sector experienced during 1994-98. Temp agencies reported that revenues for office/clerical temps, as a percent of total staffing revenues, declined from an estimated 23.9 percent in 1992 to 16.5 percent in 1998. Even though growth rates declined, the office/clerical sector experienced a 52 percent **increase in revenues** from 1992 to 1998, increasing from an estimated $8.9 billion in 1992 to $17.1 billion in 1998. The office/clerical sector outperformed every other staffing sector except for technical/IT and professional-employer organizations. In regards to **new jobs created**, the office sector contributed almost half of the 69 million jobs created from 1950 to 1995, and 59 percent of those created from 1979 to 1995. The office sector is also the fastest growing sector for total jobs available in the marketplace, comprising 41 percent of the current workforce. The **length of assignments** for temporary office/clerical assignments is increasing as well, though some experts disagree on whether the days of the short, fill-in assignment are numbered. For example, TotalTemps' senior vice president, Ben Bradley, maintains that "The old 'replacement secretary' to cover a two-week vacation order has disappeared." However, Longman Staffing Services' public relations director, Gena Rome, believes that "The days of shift fill-in assignments aren't over, but the average assignment is now for months, not days." Gone or not, though the **traditional image of the office has undergone a significant transformation** over the years, office/clerical workers remain a vital part of the workforce.

The new key terms appear at around seven to eight lines into the new paragraphs, so it is apparent that the long paragraph should be broken up into these shorter paragraphs:

During the past 40 years, the **office/clerical sector** has been the **fastest growing sector** in the marketplace. That occurred in spite of a slowdown in growth the office/clerical sector experienced during 1994-98. Temp agencies reported that revenues for office/clerical temps, as a percent of total staffing revenues, declined from an estimated 23.9 percent in 1992 to 16.5 percent in 1998.

Even though growth rates declined, the office/clerical sector experienced a 52 percent **increase in revenues** from 1992 to 1998, increasing from an estimated $8.9 billion in 1992 to $17.1 billion in 1998. The office/clerical sector outperformed every other staffing sector except for technical/IT and professional-employer organizations.

> In regards to **new jobs created,** the office sector contributed almost half of the 69 million jobs created from 1950 to 1995, and 59 percent of those created from 1979 to 1995. The office sector is also the fastest growing sector for total jobs available in the marketplace, comprising 41 percent of the current workforce.
>
> The **length of assignments** for temporary office/clerical assignments is increasing as well, though some experts disagree on whether the days of the short, fill-in assignment are numbered. For example, TotalTemps' senior vice president, Ben Bradley, maintains that "The old 'replacement secretary' to cover a two-week vacation order has disappeared." However, Longman Staffing Services' public relations director, Gena Rome, believes that "The days of shift fill-in assignments aren't over, but the average assignment is now for months, not days."
>
> Gone or not, though the **traditional image of the office has undergone a significant transformation** over the years, office/clerical workers remain a vital part of the workforce.

When you write, look at key terms in the first sentence of each of your paragraphs and key terms in the last sentences. If they are not clearly related to each other, you may have more than one idea per paragraph. Use that as a sign you should check the focus of the paragraphs in your e-mail, memo, letter, or report.

❖ Example

Looking at the key terms in the first sentence and last sentence in the next paragraph will signal to you that either the topic has changed or the writer is developing an idea from the first thought to the last. The key terms are bolded for this illustration.

> The **community's population** is 32 percent African American, 38 percent Hispanic, 28 percent White, and 2 percent Asian and other minorities. For cultural, social, and environmental reasons, African Americans and Hispanics have **higher rates of preventable health issues** from lack of immunization, heart disease, diabetes, hypertension, tuberculosis, certain cancers, and infant mortality.

The first sentence seems to indicate that this is the "community's population" paragraph. However, the second sentence doesn't fit that. It contains the "higher rates of preventable health issues" key term. The writer would have to decide whether they are two unrelated concepts requiring two different paragraphs, or whether he is building toward a conclusion. If the writer is building toward a conclusion, he must guide the reader from the first key term to the second. That requires a transition from the "population diversity" concept to the "higher rates of health issues" concept.

A transition, bolded for this example, takes care of the problem:

> The community's population is 32 percent African American, 38 percent Hispanic, 28 percent White, and 2 percent Asian and other minorities. **This diversity in population results in more residents having health issues because,** for cultural, social and environmental reasons, African Americans and Hispanics have higher rates of preventable health issues from lack of immunization, heart disease, diabetes, hypertension, tuberculosis, certain cancers, and infant mortality..

Best Practice

Write sentences that are complete, simple, clear, and straightforward.

Guidelines for this best practice:

1. Write simply.

2. Write the sentence first; then refine it.

3. Use active voice unless you have a reason to use passive voice.

4. Avoid inserting information that breaks up the sentence.

5. Write the most straightforward sentences you can.

6. Try to have only one or two concepts in a sentence.

7. Avoid putting concepts not related to each other in a sentence.

8. Never drop articles and other words as a shorthand method of writing.

Write simply.

Write as you would speak. When you read the sentences you have
written, they should sound like sentences you might speak, although
you've worked on them to eliminate fragments and deadwood. Some
business writers feel that their sentences are awkward, so they keep
revising them. One of the primary reasons they are uncomfortable with
their sentences is their belief that to sound intelligent and professional,
sentences should be long, complicated, and "businesslike." They could
eliminate the problem by writing as simply as possible.

Write the sentence first; then refine it.

Business writers sometimes become so caught up in trying to think
up a wonderful sentence that it takes several minutes just to write it. To
avoid that, write the sentences as you would speak them first. Imagine
the reader is sitting in front of you saying, "I don't understand what you
just said. Explain it to me more clearly." Write what you would say in
response. Those are the clear, simple sentences you would use when
speaking to someone.

Write all the sentences necessary to convey a single thought or point
without editing them. Then, refine the sentences to make them explicit.
You likely won't have to do very much with the text. You may have to
combine some sentences, separate some to make them clearer,
reorganize, and delete words that are deadwood. However, your first
sentences are usually good guides to what you should write.

Use active voice unless you have
a reason to use passive voice.

English verbs have two voices: active voice and passive voice. In
active voice, the person acting is clear: "The manager wrote the report
yesterday." The person acting is the manager.

In passive voice, the writer doesn't specify the person acting: "The
report was written." It could have been written by the secretary, a
manager, or Abraham Lincoln—we don't know.

The sentence is still in passive voice if the writer specifies the actor
later in the sentence: "The report was written yesterday by the manager."
The passive sentence is "The report was written."

Reasons for using active voice

Using active voice gives the reader all the facts. She can then use them as needed to make decisions and act. Passive voice keeps the identity of the actor secret or at least secret until later in the sentence. The reader can't use her knowledge of who acted to make decisions or act effectively.

❖ Example

Every sentence in this paragraph is in passive voice:

> The pipeline was inspected and was found to have cracks at three joints. The decision was made to replace the three joints and plans to take care of the problem were drawn up. However, after the work was completed, the leaks continued.

Because all the sentences are passive voice, the reader can't tell who acted. He won't know whom to ask about the inspection, who decided to replace the parts, who drew up the plans to take care of the problem, and who actually did the work to eliminate the leaks. The reader will not be able to use those important facts to take the next steps to alleviate the problem because the writer used passive voice.

Change the passive voice sentences to active voice unless you have a good reason to use passive voice:

> The supervisor inspected the pipeline and discovered cracks at three joints. The plant maintenance manager decided to replace the three joints and drew up plans to have the contracting department engage a contractor. However, after the contractor completed the work, the leaks continued.

Now the reader doesn't have to be Sherlock Holmes to know who discovered the cracks, who decided to replace them, who drew up the plans, and who did the work. When issues come up about the pipeline and what happened, the reader will more likely remember what he read and act on the information.

If you don't know who performed the action, at least refer to the group of people or the person's position:

Instead of this: It was found that 53 percent of the workers
disapproved.

Write this: The researchers found that 53 percent of the workers
disapproved.

When passive voice is appropriate

Business writers should use passive voice sparingly. You may use
passive voice when you don't know who performed the action, you want
to soften the impact by not stating who performed the action, or the
identity of the actor is unimportant.

Changing passive voice to active voice

To change passive voice to active, identify the performer of the
action. If the performer is in a "by the" phrase, move the performer to
the subject position, just before the verb.

Instead of this: The meeting was opened by the chairperson.

Write this: The chairperson opened the meeting.

If the writer did not name a performer, choose a subject that fits the
context.

Instead of this: The test results will be announced next week.

Write this: We will announce the test results next week.

The researchers will announce the test results next
week.

Avoid mixing active and passive voice in the same sentence. The
first half of this sentence is active, but the second half is passive:

We found the lost contract, and the client was notified immediately.

Instead, use active voice throughout:

We found the lost contract and notified the client immediately.

Use "I" and "you" freely

One reason business writers use passive voice is that they were
taught in school not to use "I," "you," or "we" in writing. The reason for
this archaic rule is that in the nineteenth and early twentieth centuries,
business writers learned that they should be distant from readers. Much
passive voice is an effort to avoid "I" and "you." Explicit business writing

uses "I," "you," and "we" as people normally do in speaking, without reservation, in all business documents.

If your company refuses to permit you to use "I" or "you," use words such as "this researcher" or "the researcher" to refer to your role in the activity of the document. In any event, avoid passive sentences such as "The test was administered . . ."

Don't use "one" to refer to anyone in the world: "One should not antagonize clients." It's archaic and strained.

Don't assign thought and action to inanimate things as in, "The investigation found . . ."

Avoid inserting information that breaks up the sentence.

View your sentences as a story. The writer interrupts this sentence to state information that disturbs the flow of this story:

> I had agreed to look at the data again, at our May 15 meeting in Cincinnati with you and the MIS people there, to see why it seems to indicate that the glass container division is losing money.

Always attempt to present the story in one, continuous thought. When you have other information you want to put in, place it at the beginning of the sentence before you start the thought, at the end after you finish the thought, or in a separate sentence.

> At our May 15 meeting in Cincinnati with you and the MIS people, I had agreed to look at the data again to see why it seems to indicate that the glass container division is losing money.

Usually, you can find a way to insert the additional information so it does not interrupt a sentence. When you try to find a place for it, you may find that the information is sufficiently out of place to require its own sentence, or you may discover that it is not important enough to include at all.

Write the most straightforward sentences you can.

If a sentence seems awkward to you, it will be even more awkward for the reader. Sometimes, business writers try to sound formal and professional by creating sentences they think sound more businesslike. That just creates odd sentences. Instead, use the same sentences you use when you speak, with improvements that you are able to make in writing because you can reconsider and revise. This example uses awkward sentences:

> "Tardy" is when you are more than 15 minutes late for work. Punctuality being important to successful business functioning, the company prefers that you arrive at your designated work area employing a virtue that will reward you in the long run . . . being on time.

Besides breaking a raft of usage rules, these sentences are difficult to understand because they do not state the thoughts plainly. The writer needs to use the same words she would use if she were explaining the policy to someone sitting in front of her:

> You are considered "tardy" when you are more than 15 minutes late for work. Punctuality is important for the business to function well and for your success, so the company wants you to be at work on time.

Try to have only one or two concepts in a sentence.

Usually put only one or two important concepts in a sentence. You may sometimes have three, but rarely have four or more. If you include more than three, the reader will become lost in the text. Keep sentences to an average of around 15 to 20 words.

To make the sentence clear and simple, follow this procedure:

1. Write a sentence as you would speak it.

2. Identify the main point in the sentence. It will be a noun (person, place, or thing) and an action or feeling.

3. Identify any other points by looking for the key terms. Count the number of other points.

4. If you have two or more points, including the main point, see whether any points would be clearer if they were in different sentences. However, if the sentence has two or more points that should remain together in a sentence to complete the thought and the sentence is perfectly clear, leave them in the sentence.

5. If the sentence already contains more than 15 words with two points, you likely will want to put the next point into its own sentence.

❖ Example

This sentence has two main points and three additional points. You can identify them by finding the key terms. The two main points are in two key terms: "evaluators identified double the number of bugs" and "provided more suggestions and comments." You'll see the other key terms the writer has added after the two main points.

> Compared to similar programs managed by Fallon, the **evaluators** in the Apex program **identified** more than **double the number of bugs**, provided **more suggestions and comments**, comprising **275 pieces of discrete data**, with the **level of participation** in evaluations and **producing call reports better** than those in similar programs.

Clear writing has sentences that average 15 to 20 words. This sentence contains 49 words. The two main points are in 26 words: "Compared to similar programs managed by Fallon, the evaluators in the Apex program identified more than double the number of bugs [and] provided more suggestions and comments." This sentence is confusing because the words following the two main points add three points using 23 more words. These are the other points the writer adds:

- comprising 275 pieces of discrete data

- the level of participation in evaluations was better

- the level of participation in producing call reports was better

To be explicitly clear, the writer should decide that a length of 26 words for the two main points already exceeds the limit for a clear sentence, so the sentence should break at the end of the main points. The next point, about the 275 pieces of data, probably isn't necessary, so the writer might decide simply to delete it. That leaves the last two points;

they fit naturally with each other so they should be in their own
sentence. Here is the revised version:

> Compared to similar programs managed by Fallon, the evaluators
> in the Apex program identified more than double the number of bugs
> and provided more suggestions and comments. The Apex program
> evaluators also had better levels of participation in evaluations and
> produced better call reports.

Avoid putting concepts not related to each other in a sentence.

Writers sometimes create sentences containing concepts that are not
closely related to each other. These sentences are common in newspaper
and magazine articles because they've become part of a characteristic
journalism style. However, they are simply not good writing. This is an
example:

> Founded in July 1993, the company's president is Frieda Lundgren.

The founding date is not related to the president. The writer should
break the two concepts into two sentences or rewrite the sentence to join
with other ideas:

> The company was founded in July 1993 by George Lundgren.
> Today, the president is George's daughter, Frieda Lundgren.

Never drop articles and other words as a shorthand method of writing.

Business writers sometimes drop articles ("a," "an," and "the") and
other short words when they write list items or table items because they
feel that list items and table items should be short. However, that results
in text that is difficult to understand, and the shorthand does nothing to
help readers read the list more quickly.

❖ Example

This shorthand version of a list is unclear.

Decisions:
1.   Purchase crane and associated equipment.
2.   Sell old crane....Mitchell and Associates....agreed price.
3.   Purchase training option

Write in full sentences in all of your business writing. This is the same list written with complete sentences:

We made the following decisions at the meeting:
1.   Purchase the crane and associated equipment.
2.   Sell the old crane to Mitchell and Associates at the agreed price.
3.   Purchase the training option with the new crane.

Best Practice

Use only simple punctuation.

Guidelines for this best practice:

1.   Rarely use these punctuation marks:

Dashes (— -)

Exclamation points (!)

Ellipses (. . .)

Slashes (/)

Semicolons (;)

Brackets ([ ])

2.   Use these punctuation marks freely:

Commas (,)

Periods (.)

Colons (:)
Parentheses ( )
Question marks (?)
Quotation marks (" ')

Explicit business writing uses the simplest punctuation marks because they help the reader navigate through the text most easily.

Rarely use these punctuation marks.

Some punctuation marks do not make business writing clearer. They may even cause confusion for three reasons:

1. Business writers use them in nonstandard ways so their meanings are not clear to the reader.

2. Even when used correctly, their meanings are most often lost on readers. Most readers interpret them as simply breaks in the sentence.

3. Other, simpler punctuation marks communicate more quickly and easily.

You may know how to use these punctuation marks appropriately, and they may contribute to the clarity of your writing. If so, you may decide to continue to use them. However, if you, like most business people, are not sure how to us them correctly, don't use them at all.

Dashes (— –)   Many business writers don't realize that a dash is different from a hyphen. A hyphen is a short horizontal line: (-). Use hyphens only to join words or within words. A dash is two or three times the length of a hyphen: (— and –). Use dashes to interrupt sentences and show ranges of numbers.

However, commas and parentheses are better punctuation marks to interrupt sentences. Use commas instead of dashes to insert information into the sentence because commas maintain the flow of information. Use parentheses around information that is clearly not part of the flow of the sentence.

Most business writers don't know these rules for using dashes:

1. There are two dashes: an em dash (—) and an en dash (–).

2. An em dash is the longer dash. Use an em dash to make a strong interruption in a sentence—only a strong interruption.

3. An en dash is shorter than an em dash, but longer than a hyphen. Use an en dash to show ranges of numbers: 1995–1998.

4. Don't put blank spaces before or after dashes. That likely will change in the future because publications are commonly putting spaces before and after dashes, but for now, the spaces are still not acceptable in business writing.

Exclamation points (!)

Except for use in newsletters and informal statements, don't use exclamation points in business writing. Readers expect you to be objective, so they feel uncomfortable if you express emotion, such as that suggested by an exclamation point.

Especially don't use a string of exclamation points in e-mail: "Change the date!!!!!!" Readers feel you're screaming at them and may misunderstand the feeling you're conveying. They'll assume the worst.

Ellipses (. . .)

Business writers use three to five periods in a row to show a change in thought, a pause, or other interruption in the text. However, the reader can't interpret the meaning the writer is giving to the periods, and it is a misuse of a form of punctuation called an ellipsis. An ellipsis should be three periods separated by spaces: (. . .). Use the ellipsis within a quotation to show that words have been omitted from the quotation. You may also use an ellipsis to show that a choice must be made in an "If . . . then" statement in a procedure. Otherwise, don't use the ellipsis.

Slashes (/)   Don't use slashes in business writing except in fractions or names everyone spells with slashes. They don't convey the relationship between the words separated by slashes. For example, is a supervisor/coordinator a supervisor **who is also** a coordinator, a supervisor **and** a coordinator, a supervisor **or** a coordinator, or a supervisor **also called** a coordinator? The reader isn't sure.

Substitute the word describing the relationship for the slash. Of course, if your company actually has a "supervisor/coordinator" position, you must spell that title with the slash. Don't put blank spaces before and after slashes.

Business writers often use "and/or" when "and" or "or" will suffice. If you feel the reader may be confused if you use "and" or "or" when it could be either, state that explicitly. The statement, "I will meet with your designer and/or graphic artist," would be better written in this way: "I will meet with your designer or graphic artist or both." However, "and/or" does work at rare times; just use it when you are sure it is necessary and the reader will understand it.

Semicolons (;)   Avoid using semicolons unless you know well how they should be used. Business writers use them to extend sentences or as a special code meaningful to the writer that is lost on the reader. The semicolon is often confused with the colon (:).

Semicolons may be used to separate items in a list when the list has longer items and is embedded in a paragraph. However, explicit business writing requires that lists with longer items be broken out with bullets or numbers. If you feel the need to use semicolons between items in a sentence, that is an indication that you should break the list out using numbers or bullets.

Brackets ([ ])   Don't use brackets unless your company has adopted them for some specialized use, such as around the names of keyboard keys: "Press the [Esc] key." They are another form of punctuation writers use as special notations, but their special meaning is often known only to the writer. Standard usage for brackets requires that they be limited to these uses:

1. In quotations to show that the writer has added words to clarify the quotation

2. As parentheses within parentheses in text

3. To set off phonetic symbols, such as [ä]

Use these punctuation marks freely.

Commas

Commas create clear, explicit sentences. This short explanation of how to use commas in business writing is not intended to suggest that you should not learn standard usage rules for commas. It is just that many business writers don't know the rules or don't apply them, so this advice about using commas provides a set of easy-to-apply guidelines you can use while you're learning the rules for comma usage.

Use commas to make text clearer. The comma is a signal to the reader that a small change in the text is occurring. When you believe a comma will make the writing clearer, put one in. If a comma might interrupt the flow of the sentence or might make it unclear, don't put one in.

Don't put in a comma every place you seem to pause as you say the sentence to yourself. Sometimes that makes the sentence less clear because it breaks up the thought.

To apply the guidelines that follow, start by finding the thing the sentence is about and its action. Sometimes, they're separated. The thing and action form the main part of the sentence. The main parts are bolded in these sentences:

In a moment, **we saw the car turn around.**

Before the meeting, **we introduced ourselves to the guests**.

Follow these guidelines for using commas to make the writing clear.

1. If the sentence has words that come **before** the main part, put a comma after the words to show that you've finished them and you're starting the main part of the sentence. The main parts are bolded in these examples:

    > After eating, **we listened to John speak**.

    > To our surprise, **the room was very spacious**.

2. If the sentence has words that come **after** the main part, put a comma before the words to show that you've finished the main part and are adding a thought.

    > **We finally reached the house**, totally exhausted.

    > **The car was older**, but elegant.

3. If the sentence contains two things and two actions, forming two main parts, put a comma between them to show that the first main part has ended and the next main part is beginning.

    > After we loaded the packages, the truck drove away.

    > This vendor will do for now, but we need to find a more reliable one soon.

    > The brochures didn't meet our standards, and they arrived two days late.

    > Sara and Jim arrived on time, so they saw the opening.

4. Put commas before and after information you have inserted in the middle of the sentence. Usually, the sentence would be unclear without the commas.

    > The software we purchased, which was the full version, doesn't have the functions we expected.

    > Later in the day, after the test was completed, we found that the problem was in the instrument.

    > We did find, to our surprise, that none of the switches had been turned on.

5. If you use two or more words to describe something following the words, put a comma between them to show that they each refer to the word following, not to each other.

> Bring the **large, red** binder with you to the meeting.
>
> He was a **confident, upbeat, articulate** candidate for the position.
>
> Inside the pipes were **old, worn** gaskets.

6. If the sentence has items in a list connected by "and," put a comma at the end of each item, even just before the "and."

> You should access the page, click on "Agents," and locate the agent's name in the list you see.
>
> We'll have to set up product support, fulfillment, and billing.
>
> I was pleased to see that the new version is easier to use, faster in preparing reports, less difficult to navigate, and capable of handling more customers.

Periods

Use periods at the ends of all complete sentences, even in lists. Periods are clear signals to the reader that a thought has ended.

However, don't put periods at the ends of items in lists when the items are not complete sentences. Normally, don't put periods after headings unless they are complete sentences.

Watch for run-on sentences. When you insert a comma in a longer sentence, check to see whether you really want to end the first part of the sentence with a period. If you have complete sentences before and after the comma, insert a period and make two sentences.

Watch for sentence fragments. When you put a period at the end of a short sentence, check to be sure the words before the period and the words after the period do not need to be in the same sentence.

Colons

A colon is two periods in a column (:). It is not the same as a semicolon (;), which is a comma below a period. Use colons at the ends of sentences to show that the text that follows explains or defines the words just before the colon. You must have a complete sentence before the colon. The words that follow a colon should be added information about the last concept in the sentence. After the colon, write the explaining or defining words and a period.

Parentheses

Use parentheses when the information you are inserting into a sentence won't fit into the flow of the sentence. Parentheses help make the sentence clear because they indicate that the information is important, but not part of the flow of the sentence. However, your first choice is always to use commas so the information remains part of the normal flow of the sentence. If you use parentheses often, look at the information you're putting into parentheses to see whether it could go into the sentence without the parentheses.

Question marks

Use question marks as usual. Never use a series of question marks to ask a question emphatically: "Where is the report????" It feels like you're scolding and the reader may feel you're angry.

Quotation marks

Use double quotation marks (") unless you are quoting something within a quotation: "Wei said, 'Put these on the wall' and gave Terri the posters."

Best Practice

Use words every intended reader will understand.

Guidelines for this best practice:

1. Make sure the reader understands every word in your document.

2. Use modern, everyday words and phrases rather than archaic words and phrases.

3. Use plain English.

4. Evaluate the readability of your writing.

5. Be precise in the words you use.

6. Use jargon words only when they're appropriate.

7. Include defining words to ensure that the concept is clear.

8. Use pronouns only when the text sounds awkward if you don't use them.

9. Avoid abbreviations and acronyms.

10. Avoid using legal definitions.

Your document uses words to convey to readers the concepts you have in mind. If your readers misunderstand a concept because they misunderstood a word, they may fail to achieve your business objectives.

Make sure the reader understands every word in your document.

The reader must understand every word in your document to understand your message. Be especially attentive to key terms that represent concepts. Evaluate each new key term as you write it:

1. Will the reader understand the connection between this key term and the others you have presented? You must be confident the reader understands the connection, or you must explain the

connection well enough that you are confident the reader will understand it after reading your explanation.

2. Will the reader have a working definition of the key term? If you do not feel confident the reader knows the concept the key term represents, you must either

    •   define the concept clearly enough for the reader to understand it, or

    •   replace the concept word with plain words you are sure the reader will understand.

Successful business writers understand the meanings behind the concept words well enough to be able to use simple words to define them or use simple words in place of them. Unsuccessful writers either don't understand the concepts well enough to explain them in plain words or aren't sensitive to the need to ensure that readers know the concepts behind the words. As a result, their readers often feel lost.

❖ Example

This text is intended for the users of a company's data processing system. The users are data-entry clerks unfamiliar with the inner workings of the system.

As part of the year-end maintenance procedure, I have processed the 2004 files and reports on the Datafind system. Each of the recently used folders is currently stored in the Alpha directory as well. Any leftover files from the previous year may have also been processed as appropriate.

As written, the text is difficult for a user to understand. The reader may feel that the writing is too technical, but that's not the problem. The problem is that the writer isn't helping the reader understand all of the concepts represented in the words. Here again is the text, this time with the key terms bolded:

> As part of the **year-end maintenance procedure,** I have **processed** the **2004 files and reports** on the **Datafind system.** Each of the **recently used folders** is currently **stored** in the **Alpha directory** as well. Any **leftover files** from the **previous year** may have also been **processed as appropriate.**

Some of the key terms will be obvious to the reader, such as "2004 files and reports," "Datafind system," and "previous year." However, the writer should define "year-end maintenance procedure" or decide not to use the key term. If you don't think your readers know the concept and the key term isn't necessary in the explanation, don't use the key term. Substitute the plain words that explain the concept.

The writer would make the explanation explicit for these data-entry clerks by eliminating the jargon words that were not necessary and substituting plain words for concepts the readers may not understand. The resulting explanation follows. The original, undefined key terms are in the left column. The revised text with fully defined concepts is in the right column. The key terms in the left column are bolded. Most do not appear in the right column because full explanations of the concepts substitute for them.

Original, undefined words	Fully defined concepts
*As part of the **year-end maintenance procedure,***	At the end of the year, we perform a **year-end maintenance procedure** in which we move the Datafind customer records files and reports created during the ending year into storage. Moving the files and reports into storage provides a backup and frees up space on the directory where you do your work. When we store them, we compress them so they take up less space.

*I have **processed the 2004 files and reports** on the Datafind system.*	I have just moved the 2004 Datafind customer record files and reports into storage and compressed them.
	[The vague term, "processed," is replaced by the fuller explanation of what that means. "Files" is defined more fully as "customer record files."]
*Each of the **recently used folders** is currently stored in the **Alpha directory** as well.*	Copies of the last quarter 2004 files and reports are still stored in the directory you normally use so you can access them and use them as usual.
	[The vague term, "recently used folders," is replaced with the words describing the contents of the folders. The jargon term, "Alpha directory," is replaced with plain words the user will understand: "directory you normally use."]
Any **leftover files** from the **previous year** may have also been **processed as appropriate.**	We also moved any files we found from 2003 that you have not been using for six months or more into the 2003 storage subdirectory and compressed them. If you used the 2003 files during the past six months, we left them in the directory where you do your work.
	[The vague "processed as appropriate" is replaced with a full explanation of what occurred. "Leftover files" is replaced by an explanation of what those files are. "Previous year" is replaced by "2003."]

The problem wasn't that the writing was too technical; it was that the writer didn't define concepts and provide the depth of detail this group of readers needed.

You undoubtedly notice that the text is also much longer, expanding from one paragraph to three. Some business people react to this explicit form of writing by remarking that it isn't "concise," but they really mean simply "short." They have a sense that business writing should be short regardless of the impact on communication. However, the writer must include every concept, concept definition, and concept connection the reader needs to understand the message without misunderstanding.

Determine the appropriate length for a document solely by what the reader needs, not by what the writer believes is an appropriate length. In explicit business writing, what the writer prefers is irrelevant. Length must not enter into decisions about business writing unless the reader has been the one to impose length restrictions.

Nevertheless, conciseness in business writing is important. Conciseness means thoroughly explaining the relevant concepts using the fewest, most precise words possible. The information the writer presents must

1. be limited to information relevant to the objectives and readers' needs

2. contain the essential message in as few words as possible to increase the likelihood the reader will finish and understand it

3. have a limited number of key terms that represent new concepts to minimize the possibility of confusion and allow the reader to understand the message in the shortest time with the least effort possible

4. not contain deadwood words, redundancies, and the obvious

Make your writing concise by deleting unnecessary information that doesn't help the reader understand and achieve the business objectives. However, don't strive to make it short as an end in itself.

Use modern, everyday words and phrases rather than archaic words and phrases.

Avoid archaic words and phrases people don't use in speaking any more. Spoken language is constantly changing. In the eighteenth century, "cover" referred to the paper that was folded around a letter and sealed with sealing wax. That was before people started to use envelopes. Today, no one says, "I wrapped the report in a cover and sent it to you." "Cover" has been replaced by "envelope." However, people still write "under separate cover."

Write using twenty-first century English. If you wouldn't use a word or phrase in conversation, you know that it's fallen out of use in the English language. Don't write it. A short list of such words follows to give you examples. Many similar words appear in business e-mails, memos, letters, or reports every day.

Archaic words	Twenty-first century words
as per your letter	in your letter
attached herewith	here is
awaiting your reply, we are,	[omit]
going forward	from now on
Including, but not limited to	including
enclosed please find	enclosed is
hereinafter	[omit]
in closing	[omit]
in due course	today, tomorrow, next week
it has come to my attention	I have just learned
kindly advise	let us know
permit me to say that	[omit]
please be advised that	[omit]
pursuant to	[omit]
shall	will
thanking you in advance	thank you
the undersigned	we, I
under separate cover	in another envelope
we are in receipt of	we received

| we wish to inform you | [omit] |
| yours of the 10th December | your December 10 letter |

❖ Example

Instead of this: As per our conversation of 1st February, please be advised that the undersigned shall be engaged, pursuant to the oral agreements articulated at that time, until such time as said project terminates.

Write this: As we agreed when we spoke on February 1, our company will complete the project following the specifications we discussed.

Use plain English.

Use words you might speak in ordinary conversation rather than complex words or phrases. Write "find out" instead of "ascertain" and "end" instead of "terminate."

Choose the alternatives to the right of each word or phrase in this list.

Complex, unusual words	Simple words
accelerated	sped up
advise	tell
along the lines of	like
are of the opinion	believe
ascertain	find out, learn
assistance	help
assumption	belief
commence	begin, start
consummate	close, bring about
deem	think
despite the fact that	although, though
during the course of	during

financial deficit	losing money
for the purpose of	for, to
for the reason that	because
forward	send, mail
give consideration to	consider
have need for	need
in order to	to
in view of the fact that	because, since
indicate	show
initiate	begin, start
make use of	use
multiple	several, many, more than one (but prefer the exact number)
nevertheless	but
on the occasion of	when
peruse	read, study
preceding year	last year
predicated	based on
prior to	before
reside	live
subsequent to	after
succeed in making	make
terminate	end
utilize	use
we would like to ask that	please
with reference to	about

❖ Example

Instead of this:	In order to successfully accomplish the process of assessing the content of claims, the Claims Litigation Management project team has initiated a proposal for a two-stage process we advise you to review and implement with due care.
Write this:	When you review claims, follow this two-stage process the Claims Litigation Management project team has developed.

Evaluate the readability of your writing.

Overly complex writing can confuse readers. Standard business correspondence is normally written at a tenth-grade level. That does not mean the writer is talking down to readers who have college degrees. It means only that anyone who can read at the tenth-grade level or higher could understand text written at the tenth-grade level, including Ph.D.s.

The *Wall Street Journal* is written at an eleventh-grade level. *Time* and *Newsweek* are written at eighth-grade to tenth-grade levels. *Sports Illustrated* and *People* magazine are written at sixth-grade to eighth-grade levels. This page of text is written at a tenth-grade level.

Evaluate the difficulty or grade-level of your writing by looking at the vocabulary and sentence length. For reports, if the vocabulary is simple and the average sentence length is under 20 words, then the writing is probably at an appropriate grade level for most business readers. If the vocabulary is more difficult and the writing includes some long, complex sentences, then it is probably written at a higher grade level and you may lose average readers. When in doubt, keep your writing at the simple level.

For e-mail, memos, and letters, the average sentence length will be even shorter. If the sentences are longer than an average of 15 words, then the e-mail, memo, or letter may be more difficult to read.

To make your writing so clear it cannot be misunderstood, you should write at the tenth-grade level or lower for general audiences. That means the sentences average 15 to 20 words and words average around two syllables. Choose the grade level for more sophisticated or technical readers based on your understanding of their experience and knowledge.

You also could apply one of the following readability formulas to find out what the approximate grade level is for your writing.

Use Microsoft Word's readability tests.

Microsoft Word calculates two readability scores: Flesch Reading Ease Score and Flesch-Kincaid Grade Level. Follow this procedure to have Word calculate the readability scores for your text:

1. Start up Word and open a document whose readability you would like to evaluate.

2. Click on "Tools" on the Microsoft Word main menu that has "File," "Edit," and other options on it. You will see a pulldown menu.

3. Click on "Spelling and Grammar." That commands Word to start to check the spelling and grammar in your document. You will see a window with "Spelling & Grammar" at the top.

4. Click on the "Options" button that is toward the bottom of the window. You will see a window with "Spelling and Grammar" at the top and a column of options for the way Word currently has your spelling and grammar functions set up.

5. Click in the box to the left of "Show readability statistics" so a check mark appears.

6. Click on "OK" to close the window.

7. Continue the grammar and spell check. When Word has finished the grammar and spell check for the document, you will see a shaded box with "Readability Statistics" at the top. The last two scores will be for the Flesch Reading Ease Score test and Flesch-Kincaid Grade Level test. These scores are explained in the paragraphs that follow.

Flesch Reading Ease Score

The Flesch Reading Ease Score uses a 100-point scale. The higher the score, the easier the text is to read. A score of 60 to 70 is readable by most people. Our experience is that a score of around 50 is readable by most business readers. A score below 40 is probably difficult to read.

The Flesch Reading Ease Score is based on the number of syllables in the words and lengths of sentences. You can evaluate the reading ease of your writing as you finish sentences by looking at the length of sentences and number of syllables in the words:

Length of sentences and words	Likely ease of reading
Average sentence length is 12 words or fewer. There are no words with more than two syllables.	Very easy to read. Flesch Reading Ease score of 70 to 90. You will not see a score this high in normal business writing. It would be appropriate for children's books.
Average sentence length is 15 to 20 words. Average word has two syllables.	Plain English, readable by most business readers. Flesch Reading Ease Score of 50 to 70. This is a very comfortable level of difficulty for business readers.
Average sentence length is 30 to 37 words or more. Average word has three or more syllables.	Very difficult to read. Flesch Reading Ease Score of 0 to 30. This level of difficulty is not appropriate for most business documents, even technical reports. Legal contracts can achieve a 0 score.

Most text in this book scores at between 50 and 60.

Flesch-Kincaid Grade Level Score

This score provides an approximate grade level at which a reader is able to understand the text easily. For example, a score of 8.0 means that an eighth grader likely could understand the document easily. Most business documents should be aimed at seventh- to tenth-grade levels. Technical documents written for a technical audience will have a higher grade level. The scale stops at the twelfth grade, so if a writing sample has a score of 12, it could actually be at a college or post-college reading level.

Most text in this book scores at around grade 10.

Using the results

The readability formulas provide guidelines to help you as you evaluate your writing. Don't use them as standards you try to meet. Instead, if your writing has readability scores that show it might be difficult to read, look at the words you are using and the lengths of sentences. Evaluate them based on your knowledge of the reader. Does this reader need simpler vocabulary? Are you limiting most sentences to one or two concepts, with some containing three concepts, but rarely more? Revise the text based on your evaluation.

If you are on a team that writes the same types of documents for the same types of readers, regularly evaluate writing samples together in team meetings. Evaluate them using the readability tests. Discuss the vocabulary and sentence complexity and arrive at a consensus about the difficulty level you should use with these readers.

Be precise in the words you use.

Avoid words such as "many," "some," "several," and "a few." They don't communicate clearly. Use the exact number when you know it.

Avoid words that have vague or ambiguous meanings such as "which involve," "in terms of," and "vis-à-vis." The reader needs solid meaning on which to build understanding. This e-mail communicates very little:

John needs to make adjustments in terms of the reports, which will involve heading components vis-à-vis the data.

Instead, use words that state what you mean so the reader understands your message:

John needs to change the report headings so they contain words the reader will recognize immediately. He also needs to realign the columns of data so each column of data fits under the report heading describing the data.

You can evaluate the writing by looking for strong verbs such as those that appear in the example paragraph: "change," "contain," "recognize," "realign," "fits," and "describing."

Make sure the words you use convey your meaning precisely. The words in the following sentence are too imprecise:

As many of you are aware and have participated, the agent-training team has worked with Agency Development to make training.

The "have participated" doesn't fit with "As many of you . . ." Also, the training team and Agency Development can't "make" training. They can perform training or design training. The writer should reword the statements using precise wording:

> As many of you are aware and some of you know from participating in the effort, the agent-training team has worked with Agency Development to design and deliver training.

However, the entire sentence would be shorter and easier to read if the writer deleted the unnecessary words: "and some of you know from participating in the effort."

This paragraph uses words that describe neither the concepts nor the relationships among concepts:

> For an employee to be productive and innovative while developing a career at any professional services firm, an active participation in educational programs is crucial for long-term success. One fundamental lesson is the idea of leadership and how an understanding of leadership principles can facilitate a new employee's immersion into a professional atmosphere.

The writer is using words loosely. The first sentence begins with "to be productive and innovative," explaining what an employee must do to be productive and innovative, but the sentence ends by suggesting that the comment about what the employee must do "is crucial for long-term success." In other words, the writer applies the middle part of the sentence to both the beginning and end, even though they're two different concepts.

In the second sentence, the writer calls a "lesson" an "idea." A lesson isn't an idea. The writer then uses "immersion," which means lowering into water or deeply penetrating. That isn't appropriate for the employee's entrance into a professional atmosphere. The writer meant "entrance."

When writers use words imprecisely, readers become confused, the writing sounds odd, and the writer will be judged as having cloudy thinking or being unintelligent. Be as precise as you can in your use of words.

This is the rewritten paragraph:

> Participating in educational programs enables a professional services employee to be productive and innovative while developing a career. For example, training in understanding leadership principles can help the employee work more successfully with the other professionals in the firm.

Use jargon words only when they're appropriate.

Use jargon words only if you are certain the reader understands them. However, jargon words are useful to readers who understand the jargon. Because a single jargon word can contain a number of concepts, the jargon word communicates clearly and quickly to the reader who understands the words. Besides, the person who knows the jargon words will expect you to use them to show you also know them and that you regard that person as knowledgeable. However, if you have any doubts that the reader will understand the jargon, don't use it.

Business people, lawyers, engineers, and other professionals have jargon words commonly used in their specialized disciplines. A list of business jargon words follows. If you use these jargon words, be sure the readers all agree with you about the meanings.

Some words in this list, like "input," have common meanings but also have other, jargon meanings you should be careful about. "Input the data" is fine but "Let's share some input about the issue" uses the word loosely.

action plan	at-risk
based	benchmarking
buy-In	continuum
convener	convening
consensus	consensus building
disincentive	empowerment
extrapolate	incentivize
initiative	input
leverage	learnings

logistics	linkage
operationalize	metrics
paradigm	output
stakeholders	parameter
synergy	strategize
throughput	targeting
ventures	value added

Include defining words to ensure that the concept is clear.

Sometimes, a general word is not precise enough to communicate clearly. Defining words help the reader to identify the concept you are explaining.

❖ Examples

Without defining words	With defining words
the agreement	the agreement **we signed on August 13**
the software	the software **you described in your e-mail;** the **MailSorter** software
the paralegal	the paralegal **who worked on the case with Tracy**

In explicit business writing, always include the defining words unless you know the reader doesn't need them. Add defining words when you have any doubt that the reader will understand. Two sentences follow with the defining words added. They state explicitly what the writer means.

❖ **Examples**

Instead of this:	Write this:
Tell me the details about the problem.	Tell me the details about the problem **you said you experienced on Thursday.**
For the meeting, be ready for a discussion of current issues.	For the meeting **on Tuesday,** be ready to discuss **the reason you believe the fleet should be expanded and why we should change suppliers.**

Avoid pronouns unless the text sounds awkward if you don't use them.

Pronouns are words that stand for nouns. "Jim entered the room. He quietly sat beside the door." "He" is a pronoun. It fits here because it would seem awkward to use "Jim" a second time and the reader might mistakenly think there may be two Jims: "Jim entered the room. Jim quietly sat beside the door." However, pronouns can cause confusion: "Jim and Frank entered the room, each with file folders and a box of pencils. He interrupted the meeting when they fell on the floor." The reader can't tell whether Jim or Frank was the offender and what the culprit dropped. "He" and "they" could refer to more than one noun.

The pronouns that cause business writers the most problems are "this," "that," "these," and "those," called "demonstrative pronouns." After explaining two or three issues, the writer may start a new paragraph with, "This alone may have caused the problem." The reader might not know which issue the writer is referring to using "this."

❖ **Example**

The following example is unclear because of the use of "this" in the last sentence without the defining words that would help the reader understand what "this" is.

> On June 3, the facilities manager staged a fire drill in our building. We managed to clear the building in four minutes, but the goal was to clear it in three minutes. Several employees went back to answer the phone when they heard it ringing or went back for something on their desks. Some also waited for the elevator and then remembered they shouldn't use it. This was especially a problem on the third floor because it is always the last to evacuate.

"This was especially a problem" is unclear. The reader can't tell what was especially a problem: answering the phone, going back to get something on their desks, using the elevator, or all three. The writer should have omitted the pronoun or used defining words to make the pronoun clear, as in these examples: "**Waiting for the elevator** was especially a problem . . ." or "This **failure to meet the three-minute goal** was especially a problem . . ." or "**These three actions** were especially problems . . ."

Explicit business writing avoids pronouns unless they're explicitly clear. When you see "this," "that," "these," "those," or other pronouns, especially "it," replace them with the words to which they refer unless using the words to which they refer sounds awkward.

When you do use these pronouns, follow them with defining words unless the reference is so obvious the defining words are unnecessary. Instead of "This is the reason we came," write "This **need to speak with you** is the reason we came."

Most importantly, explicit business writing never uses pronouns when the pronoun might refer to more than one thing.

❖ Example

This sentence is confusing:

> Of the two routes for our trucks, the Desmond route is very different from the Armington route because of its hills and more populated cities. That will result in saving hundreds of dollars a month in shipping expenses.

The reader can't tell whether "its" refers to the Desmond route or Armington route. The reader also can't tell whether "that" refers to the lack of hills or more populated cities, or both.

The example that follows is clearer because it replaces the pronouns with the nouns and noun phrases the pronouns stand for:

Of the two routes for our trucks, the Desmond route is very different from the Armington route because of ~~its~~ **the Desmond route's** hills and more populated cities. ~~That~~ **Traveling the Armington route** will result in saving hundreds of dollars a month in shipping expenses.

Avoid abbreviations and acronyms.

Avoid using abbreviations and acronyms unless the reader knows them well. For example, you would use "IBM" or "NASA" because those abbreviations are common knowledge. If your company referred to the employment review process as ERP and every employee knew that, you could use the abbreviation in an e-mail to an employee. However, avoid using the abbreviation in an e-mail to someone outside of the company who does not know the process unless you believe that other person needs to learn the abbreviation.

The reason for preferring the full set of words is that readers may not remember the abbreviation or may be coming into the document at a point past the definition when trying to find specific information in the document later. Besides, the full set of words has no negative effects on readers—they don't mind reading them.

If the full set of words is very long, prefer to use a shortened version for it (such as "Engleman" for the firm name "Engleman, Breighton, Dawson, and Filburton"). The shortened version provides the reader with enough of the name that she will recall the full name.

Avoid abbreviations you must explain in parentheses the first time you use them. If any reader has a less than perfect memory, you will be creating confusion because the reader may have to later browse through the earlier pages of the document to find the definition.

The sample text that follows uses abbreviations. The reader may not remember the abbreviations two pages later or may return to the document later for reference, opening it at page 5 and missing the definition on page 1.

The reason for this letter is to explain the results of our effort to use an electronic filing front-end interface (EFFI) designed to allow us to eliminate much of the paperwork involved in filing records. The key requirements for the EFFI were that it would not cause undue financial burden on the part of interested parties external to our company and that it would be easy to use. By reducing the routing of physical documents between interested parties, the EFFI would also assist the company in fulfilling its obligations under the Reduced Paperwork Requirements Initiative (RPRI).

5 pages later:

We found that the EFFI did not reduce paperwork because other paperwork was involved in completing the EFFI process. As a result, those who drafted the RPRI were consulted about whether a process such as the EFFI would be exempt from RPRI.

Instead, the writer should use a shortened version for the names, as in the following example. The names are bolded for this example:

The reason for this letter is to explain the results of our effort to use an **electronic filing front-end interface** designed to allow us to eliminate much of the paperwork involved in filing records. The key requirements for the **electronic filing interface** were that it would not cause undue financial burden on the part of interested parties external to our company and that it would be easy to use. By reducing the routing of physical documents between interested parties, the **electronic filing interface** would also assist the company in fulfilling its obligations under the **Reduced Paperwork Requirements Initiative.**

5 pages later:

We found that the **electronic filing interface** did not reduce paperwork because other paperwork was involved in completing the **electronic filing interface** process. As a result, those who drafted the **Reduced Paperwork Requirements Initiative** were consulted about whether a process such as the **electronic filing interface** would be exempt from the **Initiative.**

Using the full name or shortened versions of the longer name allows the reader to recall the full name easily without having to leaf back through the document to find the definition of the abbreviation.

Avoid using legal definitions.

Avoid using the definitions such as "Company" for a firm's name or "Plaintiff" for a person's name. These are called "legal definitions" because they are used extensively in legal writing.

A growing number of businesspeople, attorneys, judges, engineers, and others whose disciplines commonly use unnecessarily complex language have joined forces to form the "plain English movement." They are encouraging all professionals to use language anyone can understand. Lawyers, especially, must understand that using conventions such as legal definitions makes their writing unnecessarily unclear. We recommend that you not write text such as the following example:

> This letter is in response to your request for a preliminary proposal for providing programming services to Beckwith, Trainer, and Associates, Inc. (hereinafter "Company"). Pivotal Programming, Inc. (hereinafter "Vendor") will create a record-keeping system for use by agents of Company at their regional offices. Vendor will design, program, and test the program over a period of six months, beginning after the contract between Company and Vendor is signed.

Instead, use the complete name or a shortened version of the name, as in this rewritten version:

> This letter is in response to your request for a preliminary proposal for providing programming services to Beckwith, Trainer, and Associates, Inc. Pivotal Programming, Inc. will create a record-keeping system for use by agents of Beckwith at their regional offices. Pivotal will design, program, and test the program over a period of six months beginning after the contract between Beckwith and Pivotal is signed.

If you wish, include the shortened version of the name in parentheses after the longer version to let the reader know you will use the shortened version in the remainder of the document. However, most often that isn't necessary.

Chapter 10

Explicit business writing has correct usage (grammar, punctuation, and spelling) and uses clear formatting.

Best Practice

Polish and proofread all documents.

Guidelines for this best practice:

1. Proofread every document, including e-mails.
2. For very important documents, proofread a printed copy, not just the onscreen text.
3. Focus when you proofread. Have a proofreading mindset.
4. Use Word's spell checker and grammar checker.

Proofread every document, including e-mail.

Proofread every document you send out. That includes e-mails. Readers judge writers' intelligence and education based on the correctness of the writing. If you send out writing that consistently has errors in it, your team members, managers, clients, and vendors will believe you're uneducated, unintelligent, imprecise, careless, and incompetent. On the other hand, if your writing is consistently clear, well organized, and correct, they'll assume you're educated, intelligent, precise, careful, and competent.

A document with no errors affects the reader in two other ways as well:

1. It helps give the document legitimacy and a professional quality.

2. It avoids the problem of having readers become so distracted by errors that they miss the message.

For very important documents, proofread a printed copy, not just the onscreen text.

If an e-mail contains important information you are sending to a reader who will be affected by errors in content or grammar, print out a copy and proofread the printed copy. For documents you will send to readers in a print form, proofread the printed copy that you will actually send to the reader. If it contains sensitive information, have someone else proofread it also to make sure the information is correct.

Double-check all numbers.

If your document contains phone numbers, dates, room numbers, or other numbers, double check them to be sure they're accurate. For phone numbers with which you aren't familiar, call the phone numbers in the text.

Identify the worst errors for your business and proofread specifically for them.

Your business should identify the worst errors that might appear in documents. If you are writing letters to prospects, correct spelling of the prospects' names is important; your phone number for contact is also important. If you are in an accounting firm, errors in figures would reflect badly on your business. If your company provides specifications to a tool-and-die company for your customers' machinery, errors in the specifications would be the worst errors.

Do a separate proofread for your company's worst errors. You may even have someone else double-check all documents for those errors.

Focus when you proofread.
Have a proofreading mindset.

When you proofread, have a proofreading mindset. In a proofreading mindset, you focus on reading more carefully than you normally read. You will be proofreading for only a few minutes, so you can expend the extra mental energy it takes to concentrate on proofreading.

1. **Eliminate distractions.** Turn off the radio or other distraction. Close your door and turn off your phone if you are proofreading an important document. If someone interrupts you, don't continue proofreading as you speak or while the person waits. Stop, take care of the interruption, and return to proofreading.

3. **Read difficult text aloud.** If some text is difficult to follow, read it aloud to see whether it contains the content you want it to have. Revise it if you detect a problem.

4. **If you change the text, proofread the changes.** Errors easily creep into text changed during editing and proofreading. Since you have just proofread the document, it seems that an error in a little change wouldn't occur. It often does.

5. **If a sentence seems unclear, change it.** As you proofread, if you read a sentence and get the wrong idea from it the first time you read it, change the sentence. Don't leave it as is because you figure out what it really means the second time you read it. The fact that you had trouble with it the first time means the reader probably will have trouble with it.

6. **Proofread every letter and space in the e-mail, memo, letter, or report.** Examine every part carefully: the subject line, title, headings, tables, page numbers, running heads, and all other text in the document. Start in the upper left corner of the screen or printed page and end in the lower right corner. Do not skip around in the document. Follow it from beginning to end.

Use Word's spell checker and grammar checker.

The spell checker compares the sequence of letters between spaces with words it has in a dictionary stored within the word processing system. It also checks a personal dictionary containing words you use that are not in the main dictionary. You have put them into the personal dictionary at some point. If the spell checker does not find the sequence of letters in its dictionary or your personal dictionary, it flags the word and gives you options for correcting it if you wish. That doesn't mean the word isn't appropriate or isn't spelled correctly. It just means it didn't find the letters in that sequence in either of its dictionaries. You have to make the final decision about whether the word is acceptable.

Set the spell checker and grammar checker to check spelling and grammar as you type.

Microsoft Word has a function that checks spelling and grammar as you type. That is useful because you will catch most spelling or grammar mistakes immediately after you have typed them so you can take care of the error. This immediate prompting may also act as a tutor, teaching you the correct spelling or grammar so you remember it next time.

After you type a word and press the space bar, Word will compare the sequence of letters in the word with the words in its dictionaries. If it can't find the sequence of letters, it will place a red squiggly line under the word to alert you that the word may be spelled incorrectly. Place your mouse cursor over the word and click with the right mouse button. You will see a pulldown menu. These are the options on the pulldown menu:

- **A list of possible alternative spellings**. Click on the correct spelling if you see it there. Word will replace the misspelled word with that correctly spelled word.

- **Ignore All** – Word will ignore this word every time it identifies it in this document.

- **Add to Dictionary** – Word will put this word into your personal dictionary so it accepts it as spelled correctly every time it encounters the word in the future in any document. Use this for names and specialized vocabulary.

- **AutoCorrect** – Choose this option to have Word change a misspelling to the correct spelling automatically every time you misspell it in the same way. To put a misspelling you often type in AutoCorrect, click on "Tools" on Word's main menu and click on "AutoCorrect Options." Type the incorrect spelling in the left column of the window and the correct spelling in the right column. Click on "OK." AutoCorrect will correct it automatically from then on, in any document you write.

- **Language** – Click on "Language" to change the language dictionary you want Word to use. Word contains dictionaries for different languages. For example, the British dictionary will not flag "emphasise" or "colour" but the American dictionary will. Set the dictionary for the language or dialect of English you are writing.

- **Spelling** – This option shows the "Spelling" options window so you can make other selections pertaining to spelling.

Word will also perform a grammar check. Word looks at the sequence of words in your text and compares it with sequences it has in a database. If the sequence you typed might have a grammar problem, Word will place a green squiggly line below it to signal you to check it. Don't change the text every time you see the green squiggly line. Evaluate the text and change it only if you see a problem.

Follow this procedure to set the spell checker to check spelling automatically as you type and set the grammar checker to check grammar as you type.

1. On Word's menu across the top of the screen, click on "Tools."

2. Click on "Options." You will see a window with tabs across the top.

3. Click on the tab titled "Spelling & grammar."

4. Make sure Word has check marks in "Check spelling as you type," "Check grammar as you type," and "Check grammar with spelling."

5. Click on "OK" to close the window.

If you are in a specialized field such as medicine or law, type a list of the words you use that are so unusual they are not in Word's dictionary. Word will put red squiggly lines under each as you type the word. Check to be sure you have spelled the word correctly; then click on it with the right mouse button and click on "Add to Dictionary" to add it to your personal dictionary. If you have co-workers who also use the words, create a master list in Word and share the file among you. Have each person open the file in Word. The list of words will have red squiggly lines under them. Each person can then add the words to his personal dictionary by right-clicking on each word and clicking on "Add to Dictionary."

Always do a manual check for spelling to identify words that are spelled incorrectly, but the incorrect spelling is a word that is in the dictionary. The dictionary does not flag words that are in the dictionary but spelled incorrectly in your text. For example, the word processor would not flag any of the words in this sentence: "Eye cam too sea ewe two day." Every word is in the dictionary.

Also don't assume that the grammar checker has identified every problem with usage in your writing. Examine your sentences carefully to make sure they are clear and correct.

Best Practice

Use formatting that makes the text easy to read.

Guidelines for this best practice:

1. Use a clear, standard font.

2. Use a readable font size.

3. Use uppercase (capitals) and lowercase (small letters) as you would in a formal letter.

4. Use standard one-inch margins for printed documents.

5. Don't use full justification.

6. Use bolding, underlining, and italics sparingly.

7. Write out dates.

Explicit business writing requires that you use the most readable text formatting possible. Business writers have fallen into some conventions that may actually slow reading or impede understanding, but the conventions have become part of the corporate culture. However, our sole concern must be communicating with 100 percent accuracy to 100 percent of the readers 100 percent of the time. The text formatting conventions you use must support that goal.

Use a clear, standard font.

Fonts are divided into two categories: serif and sans serif.

This is Times New Roman, a serif font.

A serif font has little decorations on it instead of just straight lines, making the text easier to read because it forms a more distinct silhouette for a word. The most commonly used serif fonts are Times New Roman, New Century Schoolbook, Bookman, and Palatino Linotype. The main text of this book is in Palatino Linotype, a serif font.

This is Arial, a sans serif font.

The sans serif fonts have letters that make the words look like blocks because they use no decorative lines. That makes the text more difficult to read because the silhouettes of the words are less distinctive. The most commonly used sans serif fonts are Arial, Helvetica, Verdana, and Letter Gothic. The examples in this book are in Franklin Gothic Book, a sans serif font very similar to Arial.

Use a standard font such as Arial or Times New Roman for the body text. However, prefer to use a sans serif font such as Arial for the title and headings, and use a serif font such as Times New Roman for the body text. Times New Roman is easier to read because of the serifs.

Don't use two serif or two sans serif fonts in the same document.

Use a readable font size.

Usually use 11-point or 12-point font for business documents, except for headings. A font smaller than 11 points may be difficult to read. Despite some business writers' desire to keep text to one page by using a small font or narrow margins, having the text on one page has no benefit for readers, and the smaller font and more dense text within narrow margins can make reading more difficult.

Use uppercase (capitals) and lowercase (small letters) as you would in a formal letter.

In all business writing, use uppercase and lowercase as you would in a formal letter. Text written in all capitals is more difficult to read. The eye needs the unique silhouette words have when they are both uppercase and lowercase to identify the words as the reader scans the text at 250 or 300 words per minute. A sentence in all capitals looks like a jumble of lines with no clear silhouette. As a result, people read words with all capitals 10 percent slower than words with both uppercase and lowercase.

Occasionally type words using all uppercase for headings or for emphasis, but avoid writing sentences in uppercase.

Use standard one-inch margins for printed documents.

Use one-inch margins all around for business documents. You may have an additional .25-inch border on the edge of the paper where you will bind a report.

Don't use full justification.

Full justification refers to stretching the lines of text out to the right margin so paragraphs have a block look, as they do in a magazine or newspaper. However, full justification is more difficult to read because the reader's eye needs the ragged (in and out) right margin to know when the lines break. Full justification also makes the writing look like a form letter and creates varying, sometimes odd, spaces between words as the word processor adds space to stretch the text to the margin.

Some businesses started using full justification when their word processing systems permitted them to do so, presumably because they believe it makes the text look more official or professional. However, it provides no benefit for readers and has real drawbacks, so if you wish to write as explicitly as possible, don't use full justification.

Use bolding, underlining, and italics sparingly.

Use bolding, underlining, or italics only when you have a good reason to use them and the reader will understand your use. Otherwise, avoid using them.

Bolding   If overused, bolding quickly loses its benefit of showing emphasis. When entire sentences are bolded, the writer seems to be shouting. Use bolding for headings, some conventions (such as showing names of clickable buttons on a screen), and occasional emphasis. However, do not use bolding for a special code you have originated (such as bolding position titles, participant names, or special words). Readers may not get the idea and may become annoyed by the intrusive bolding.

Underlining   Underlining is difficult to read because the line interferes with seeing the letters. Use underlining very sparingly. It is appropriate only when bolding would not be suitable. Never use underlining with bolding or words in all caps. The combination of underlining and either bolding or words in all caps makes the text appear cluttered and difficult to read.

Before the advent of word processors, writers underlined publication titles to signal to the typesetter that the underlined words should be typeset in italics. Now that we can produce italics in our word processing systems, writers italicize publication titles.

Italics   Use italics for titles of publications that stand alone (books, newspapers, booklets, and so on), for foreign words or unusual words, and occasionally for emphasis or to make sentences stand apart. However, italics are also difficult to read. When you are referring to a word as a word, use quotation marks.

Write out dates.

Don't write dates as numbers (11/12/05). Some people do not know the month numbers and any businessperson could confuse the month and day when glancing at the numbers. Some countries use the convention of placing day, month, and year, so there may be confusion in today's global marketplace. The normal date format (November 12, 2005) communicates very clearly, so to write as explicitly as possible, write out dates.

PART 3

Aids for Making Explicit Writing
Part of the Company's or Agency's
Infrastructure

Chapter 11

Advice for managers who want employees to write explicit business documents

Your employees can learn to write explicit e-mails, memos, letters, and reports. The result will be that you will have a better functioning team or department, a more successful business, and less of the frustrating confusion that commonly results from poor business writing today. However, it requires that you be diligent in rewarding employees for their successes and in helping them remedy their deficiencies.

What you must do to improve your employees' writing

For your employees to have the commitment to quality writing that will result in an effective communication infrastructure in your company or agency, you must perform the following seven actions:

1. Have clear standards for writing competence that all employees know. The standards must be characteristics of business writing that focus exclusively on writing explicitly, presented as standards you can identify and evaluate. You may want to adopt the standards presented in this book.

2. Don't focus on peripheral conventions that have little or no effect on clarity of writing. They distract from the central focus of writing to communicate clearly. Don't worry about split infinitives, ending sentences with prepositions, use of "that," and all of the other usage rules that don't affect clarity.

3.   You must have competency-based training in the standards. All
     trainees must demonstrate mastery of the skills that result in
     every one of the characteristics of explicit business writing. That
     will take time. Your training program must be measured in
     months or years.

4.   The training must be individualized to address the different
     needs employees have for writing training. In the lists of
     standards presented in this book, the numbers for pages
     containing explanations of the best practices are printed beside
     the standards. A trainer can evaluate an employee's writing and
     provide a copy of the standards with the best practices the
     employee needs to work on marked. The employee can then
     read the explanation of the best practices and demonstrate the
     skills.

5.   You must follow up the training with evaluations of employees'
     writing competence and periodically solicit feedback from
     readers about each employee's writing.

6.   You must encourage employees to give each other both positive
     and negative feedback about the writing they receive.

7.   You must be willing to go through the training and evaluation of
     your writing yourself so you model clear, explicit writing. Ask
     your subordinates for feedback about your writing so you model
     being willing to ask for and receive criticism.

You must require explicit writing in e-mail.

Overly casual, unclear, poorly written business e-mail messages are
not acceptable. Businesses have become so accustomed to slovenly
e-mail that it's difficult to think of having e-mail become a writing
medium as carefully structured as letters and reports. However, all
business e-mail messages must meet the same standards we hold for
memos, letters, and reports. Here's why:

1.   E-mail has become the primary method of communicating in
     businesses, so it is the pervasive infrastructure on which all
     businesses base their day-to-day activities. Miscommunication
     creates frustration and potential failures within the system.
     Meeting the standards for explicit communication ensures that
     all e-mail messages communicate clearly.

2. Allowing informal writing for some e-mails while requiring explicit, formal writing for important ones will require writers to assess the importance of the e-mail to the reader and adjust the writing accordingly. However, writers cannot assess accurately whether the reader needs an explicit e-mail. The chance for error is too great to permit both informal and explicit e-mail. All e-mail must be formal and explicit.

3. Having standards demonstrates a clear expectation for quality in all documents, creating consistent standards that are easier to teach and adhere to.

4. Requiring explicit writing in all media, including e-mail, avoids confusion. All in the company, and especially new employees, will know that every document must communicate to 100 percent of the readers 100 percent of the time. No writing is exempt.

You will receive resistance to requiring explicit writing in e-mails, so you must have an organization-wide requirement. E-mail must not be an exception to the requirement that all business documents be written to communicate with 100 percent accuracy.

Workshops alone cannot teach writing skills.

Sending your employees to a workshop to learn writing skills is like sending a novice tennis player to a tennis workshop expecting that he will be able to compete at Wimbledon the following week. Competence in writing can be acquired only over time with regular training, practice, feedback from an instructor and the readers, and competency-based evaluations of writing ability.

Your goal must be to have all your employees write so explicitly that all readers understand their messages with 100 percent comprehension 100 percent of the time. Training to competence requires any combination of training time, practice activities, and feedback the person needs. You must not restrict the training to a number of hours, days, or weeks. It must continue as long as necessary for the person to learn the skills and demonstrate competence. You might kick off the training with a workshop, but follow with extensive training over time.

Competence in grammar should be a secondary goal.

Improper grammar usage is highly resistant to training because most of a person's written language results from deeply ingrained habits of spoken language. If the employee comes from a background that speaks a dialect of English that diverges greatly from what is considered correct usage, or has learned English as a second language, her writing will contain usage that matches the nonstandard spoken dialect or the influence of the nonnative speaker's original language. You will find it very difficult to change nonstandard usage of English to correct usage. That person must be willing to undergo training with an instructor who works with the employee's own writing samples over a long period of time, and she must be dedicated to learning the patterns of correct usage as a second language, even if she is a native speaker of English.

Workshops cannot teach correct grammar. Classroom training, drills, and instruction in grammar rules without individualized work based on the employee's writing will not teach correct grammar. Only the individualized training with an instructor evaluating the employee's writing and helping the employee learn correct usage over time will result in using correct grammar consistently.

Leave training in grammar as a secondary goal. Focus first on having employees write explicitly.

You can learn more about teaching grammar on The Business Writing Center's Web site at http://explicit.businesswriting.com.

Some guidance for upper-level administrators: You are creating an infrastructure.

When you adopt standards for writing, have your staff trained in the skills, and require quality writing, you are creating a communication infrastructure that will enhance all business operations at every level. The change from having a lack of standards and quality in business writing to having a successful communication infrastructure is analogous to changing communication from a manual typewriter to wireless data transfer. The result will be enhanced business performance every day in every document. You will see a tangible result to which you could assign a dollar figure.

The communication infrastructure will create enhanced readers as well as writers. When all employees know the standards, they will read more effectively. That means reading will be more accurate and successful, just as writing is, doubling the effectiveness of the communication infrastructure.

Frustration and errors from miscommunication will diminish. The same high standards now adopted for quality-control initiatives will be possible for business communication because the standards make quality-control measures feasible.

Achieving this infrastructure will require diligence and a willingness to overcome obstacles. Many business people will oppose such a structure because it will require them to follow strict standards in an area they have experienced as free and unstructured. However, changes in thought and the accompanying performance often require tearing down walls to build new structures. The results will be well worth the struggle.

This book is available for you to customize for your company or agency.

You may obtain the original electronic files for this book to customize for your company and print for employee use. The Business Writing Center will also customize the book for your agency or company. Access the *Explicit Business Writing* Web page at http://explicit.businesswriting.com for more information.

Chapter 12

Explicit business writing job aid

This job aid is based on the standards for explicit business writing. If you use it as a guide when you write, over time, the practices will become part of your skill set. The job aid is an on-the-job training tool that will help you learn the skills while you create business writing that is so clear it cannot be misunderstood.

The page numbers for the best practices used to meet each standard are listed to the right of the standards.

Plan, Make Notes, and Organize the Notes.   **45**

1. Decide on your objectives.   46

2. Identify the following for each reader: 48

    - knowledge of the subject
    - educational background
    - technical level
    - concreteness needed
    - depth needed

3. Write notes for everything the reader must know, using key terms. If you're responding to a request, write the person's key terms from the request.   61, 67

    Critical questions:
    - Are you providing everything the readers need? If not, add what they need.
    - Do you have anything readers don't need? If so, delete it.

4. Number the notes to show their levels.   67

Proofread critically.   **257**

PART 4

Standards for Explicit Business Writing

Business writing requires its own set of standards, distinct from journalism, creative writing, and all other forms of writing. The standards that follow are derived from the best practices presented in this book. It is recommended that companies adopt these standards, train employees to achieve them, and evaluate employee writing to ensure that the standards are being met.

The standards are in four forms:

- A set of standards for creating a cooperative atmosphere and fostering a corporate climate that values writing

- A summary set of standards for explicit business writing

- A set of detailed standards for explicit business writing

- A set of detailed standards for explicit business e-mail

To the right of each standard is the number of the page on which the best practice that results in attaining the standard is explained. Use the list of standards for individualized training.

You may create your own standards using these as templates and distribute them freely, without special permission from the author. Word files containing the standards are available free from The Business Writing Center's Web site at http://explicit.businesswriting.com. If you use these standards as they are here or in an adapted form, you must include one of these statements on the first page:

> R. Craig Hogan, Ph.D., *Explicit Business Writing: Best Practices for the Twenty-First Century* (Normal, Illinois: The Business Writing Center, 2005).

Or,

Adapted from The Business Writing Center's Standards
for Business Writing (R. Craig Hogan, Ph.D., *Explicit
Business Writing: Best Practices for the Twenty-First
Century* [Normal, Illinois: The Business Writing Center,
2005]).

Chapter 13

Standards for creating a cooperative atmosphere and fostering a corporate climate that values writing

To have a successful, viable communication infrastructure, a company or agency must

1. encourage and reward writing that is congenial and partnering

2. create a corporate climate that values writing by rewarding good writing

3. encourage employees to comment freely on the quality and content of each other's writing

4. call attention to unacceptable writing

5. offer individualized training when needed to improve employee competence and performance

6. encourage dialogue about writing

Accomplishing these goals requires that the company have clear expectations for these activities embodied in a set of standards. The standards for creating a cooperative atmosphere and fostering a corporate climate that values writing follow.

Standards for a cooperative
atmosphere that values writing

Chapter 14

A summary set of standards for explicit business writing

A short set of standards that summarizes all of the detailed standards follows. The standards apply to e-mails, memos, letters, and reports, although they will be applied differently depending on the type of document.

Standards for explicit documents

Reader Suitability

___ The document suits the readers.	45-61
___ The document gives readers everything they need or request, under the conditions they specify.	61-67, 69-71

Organization

___ The document is organized to maximize reader understanding.	67-69, 72-75

Introduction

___ The subject line and introduction explain everything readers need to be able to understand why they are receiving the document and what is in the document.	91-99, 105-110

___ Actions the reader is expected to perform, critical
information the reader must remember, conclusions,
and recommendations are presented at the
beginning of the document and explained clearly.   100-104

Body Explanations

___ The information is in clearly defined information
blocks that are marked with visual devices and
explicit opening statements.   112-129, 143-156

___ Shorter lists are broken out with numbers
and bullets.   129-143

___ The document contains complete explanations
with evidence for conclusions.   165-168, 183-205

___ Requests, problems, and issues are described
clearly, precisely, and unambiguously.   168-171

___ The document uses key terms consistently, and all
intended readers understand them.   171-178

___ Every part of the document is focused.   178-182

Style and Writing

___ The writing is concise.   208-215

___ The document has clear paragraphs, sentences,
and words the intended readers understand.   216-256

Conclusion

___ The document ends with a conclusion and
feedback loop, when appropriate, to ensure that
readers achieve the business objectives.   157-163

Editing, Proofreading, and Formatting

___ The document is polished and proofread, with
no usage errors.   257-262

___ The formatting makes the text as readable
as possible.   262-266

Chapter 15

Detailed standards for explicit business writing

The standards apply to e-mails, memos, letters, and reports, although they will be applied differently depending on the type of document.

Standards for explicit documents

The document provides readers with everything they need to achieve the writer's business objectives.

___ Topics are presented in the same order throughout
and all the contents in each part are linked.   72

The document has explicit introductions to the explanations.

___ The e-mail subject line uses words that alert the
reader to the contents, required action, or critical
information in the e-mail.   72

___ The introduction explains everything readers need
to know to be able to understand why they are
receiving the document.   94

___ The introduction contains actions the reader is
expected to perform and critical information the
reader must remember.   100

___ The document includes conclusions and
recommendations in a summary at the beginning.   101

___ A clear statement of the contents is included at the
end of the introduction.   105

The document has a clear framework that guides readers through the information.

___ The information is in clearly defined
information blocks.   112

___ Each information block has an explicit opening
statement.   118

___ Longer lists have an opening statement of the
contents and explicit openings for list items.   123

___ Shorter lists are broken out with numbers and
bullets.   129

___ The document is presented in a clear visual
blueprint so readers can see the organization as
they read.   143

___ Tables are used to organize matrix data.   154

The document contains explanations that are so clear they cannot be misunderstood.

The document has clear, concise paragraphs, sentences, and words.

The document has well-written sentences, correct usage, and clear formatting.

Chapter 16

Standards for explicit business e-mail

The e-mail follows protocol to ensure that e-mail remains a viable medium for business communication.

The e-mail provides readers with everything they need to achieve the writer's business objectives.

__ The e-mail gives readers everything they need to be
successful in achieving the business objective, with
no unnecessary information.   54

__ An e-mail responding to a request provides what the
requester asked for, under the conditions the
requester specified.   61

__ Readers receive information at the specific points
where they need it for maximum understanding.   67

__ When readers have differing needs or abilities,
different versions or sections of the e-mail match the
readers' needs and abilities.   69

__ The e-mail presents topics in the same order
throughout and links all the contents in each part.   72

The e-mail has explicit introductions to the message.

__ A subject line alerts the reader to the contents,
required action, or critical information in the e-mail.   92

__ The e-mail begins with a salutation.

__ The introduction explains everything readers need
to know to be able to understand why they are
receiving the e-mail now.   94

__ The introduction contains descriptions of any
actions the reader is expected to perform and critical
information the reader must remember.   100

__ If the e-mail contains conclusions and
recommendations, they are in a summary at
the beginning.   101

__ A clear statement of the contents is provided at the
end of the introduction.   105

**The e-mail has a clear framework that guides readers through
the information.**

__ Content is in clearly defined information blocks.   112

**The e-mail contains explanations that are
so clear they cannot be misunderstood.**

The e-mail has clear, concise paragraphs, sentences, and words.

**The final draft of the e-mail has well-written
sentences with correct usage.**

**The e-mail messages help develop cooperation, continuous
enhancement of writing, and expectations for quality.**

Index